Inner Acceptance

How to Embrace Your Inner Mind
and Change Your Life

Shannon Mosher

Blue Kokua Press

Inner Acceptance: How to Embrace Your Inner Mind and Change Your Life

By Shannon Mosher
Copyright © 2020 Shannon Mosher
Blue Kokua Press
1306 Kingwood Dr. Ste C
Kingwood, Tx 77339

Publisher's Note

This publication is designed to provide accurate and authoritative information in regard to the subject matter covered. It is sold with the understanding that the publisher is not engaged in rendering psychological, financial, legal, or other professional services. If expert assistance or counseling is needed, the services of a competent professional should be sought.

Cover design by Kerry Watson

Edited by Stephanie Lee Mira

All Rights Reserved.

All rights reserved. No part of this publication may be reproduced, distributed, or transmitted in any form or by any means, including photocopying, recording, or other electronic or mechanical methods, without the prior written permission from the author, except in the case of brief quotations embodied in critical reviews and certain other non-commercial uses permitted by copyright law.

First Printing: September 2020

ISBN-13: 978-1-7356026-0-8

About the Author

Shannon Mosher's lifelong motivation has been to help others redefine themselves and discover true joy and meaning in life. She has a master's degree in counseling from Liberty University with background in hypnotherapy and executive-level leadership. Shannon is a licensed mental health professional committed to helping her clients take control of their lives.

Shannon Mosher is an ICBCH Certified Professional Hypnotist, a Licensed Professional Counselor-Intern under the supervision of Dr. Marty Lerman, and an expert in helping people create lasting change. She actively participates in podcasts on Grow Perspective: LifeSpring Radio, and has grown an audience of people who are inspired by her work.

Do you want Shannon Mosher to be the keynote speaker at your next event? Call (832) 543-3002 or email us at info@inneracceptance.com

Why Read This Book

There is no more straightforward way to make significant changes in your life than by learning inner acceptance. This book reveals the meaning of your inner thoughts or "parts" development, how they interact with each other and affect your behavior, and the power of accessing true inner acceptance. You may find yourself at times feeling like you are not good enough or unlovable, and your future will always be doomed. Nothing lasts forever, and reading this book is taking the first step into your journey of inner healing, compassion, awareness, and self-acceptance. Your past does not define you, nor should you be terrified of your future.

Exploring your inner world is a mystery to most, yet this book offers the key you have been waiting for that unlocks the door to discovering your inner power and living a life of significance. Inner acceptance can help you overcome struggles and step into a new chapter of your life.

In this book, Shannon reveals strategies that actually work and teaches you how to apply them on your own. She also shares stories of actual case studies for readers to connect and relate to. When you are finished with this book, you will have a new resource that you can tap into for the rest of your life.

Access free resources and guided meditations from this book at www.inneracceptance.com

Are you ready to understand the WHY behind your feelings and behavior?

Curious about how you can turn feeling misunderstood into validation and encouragement?

Inside is a step-by-step guide backed by research that is easy to follow, ensuring you take the steps you need to make changes at your pace, and with confidence.

Start making daily changes in your life with our Gratitude Sprinkles journal! Get your copy at www.bluekokua.com.

Acknowledgements

I thank my incredibly supportive husband, Steven. Our four amazing children, Chloe, Joshua, Gabriel, and Matthew. My father, John, and my sister, Rene. My truly beautiful-minded friends, Christy Kössler and Deanna Uldall.

Your encouragement enabled me to offer a book that will change the lives of many people!

Table of Contents

Introduction 1

Chapter 1: How Inner Parts Develop 9

Chapter 2: Your Inner World 23

Chapter 3: The Unconscious Mind 40

Chapter 4: Opening the Door of Your Mind 51

Chapter 5: Accessing Acceptance 61

Chapter 6: Creating Inner Dialogue 71

Chapter 7: Your Wise Self 79

Chapter 8: Reframing Your Thoughts 87

Chapter 9: Great Expectations 100

Chapter 10: Seeking Further Guidance 108

Conclusion 113

Inner Acceptance

Introduction

If you can give up your desire to always experience pleasant things, at the same time as giving up your fear of experiencing unpleasant things, then you'll have a quiet mind.
—Andy Puddicombe

Let's face it. Life is complicated. Sometimes, you are ahead of the game and feel like a champion on a podium. Other times, it feels like you're running a race that has no finish line. And then there are the times when you train and train to run the race, but never seem to qualify.

Yes, life is complicated, but it has a way of telling us exactly where we need to be.

You can have meaningful and fruitful experiences by opening your mind and listening to what's inside you. Too often, we get caught up in the noise around us or forget how to be comfortable with just ourselves. But in those moments when we truly listen, we invite ourselves to accept who and where we are, moving us beyond the fear, worry, doubt, and anger that might prevent us from being who we want to be. Over time, this inner acceptance will reveal insights that positively impact how you feel about the present and how you view your future.

As a mental health therapist and clinical hypnotherapist, I've created this book to help you to get to know yourself better by learning about your inner "parts." Your inner parts are also commonly referred to as the voices inside your mind. Throughout, I will encourage you to honor and embrace every part of who you are—even those parts that seem negative—so you can discover your own personal inner acceptance. You'll learn how to become curious and examine your inner parts and get to know them better. This inner awareness places the pieces of your unique puzzle together so you can access self-approval and acceptance. Instead of looking outside yourself or to others to find approval or a sense of value, you will learn how to turn inward and see the value inherent in who you are.

Now, I understand that it seems like a tall order. Something inside of you is probably scoffing and saying, "Whatever, lady! I think it's time to read another book." If so, good! This book is for you!

You have fascinating and magnificent parts in you that have a history, a story, and a role they play in your life.

Inner Acceptance

Psychologists and hypnotherapists have created theories to make sense of these different parts, and I'll make use of them to help you better understand how your inner parts impact your life and either move you toward or away from your goals.

As you read this book, you may notice yourself drifting into your thoughts or replaying images of old memories in your head. If so, it means what you are reading is resonating and is starting to work for you. I know it may be difficult to think about events in your past, but my goal is not to make you relive painful moments again and again. Instead, I'll teach you how to access those memories in such a way that they do not overwhelm you. Then, you can learn from them and eventually heal from the burdens these memories hold.

When I was a kid, I often told myself I was not good enough. I believed that I was the black sheep of the family, partly because of the things my father used to say. You see, my parents were teen parents. My mother was 16 when she gave birth to my older sister, and she was 18 when she had me, while my father was 21. They both dropped out of school, and I assume because of the embarrassment and shame, my father developed a negative core belief about himself that later became mine.

We moved from house to house, partly because my parents had difficulty holding down jobs. I found myself comparing my life to those of others, internalizing a deep sense of embarrassment, self-contempt, and shame along the way. My friends and their families seemed to have their lives all put together, but mine wasn't. At times, I felt like I shouldn't even hang around well-off people because they'd eventually figure out how poor and unfortunate I was. Deep down, I really wanted my life to be just like theirs.

Thus began my quest to seek approval from everyone. I believed that if I pushed harder in school, then maybe others would accept me. Perhaps, working hard could prove to others that I could be more than my irresponsible parents. Instead, they would see me as someone worthy of their acceptance because I worked hard and made good decisions. But I needed recognition from my family too, as the only time I ever received attention from my family was when I was first in class or made the honor roll. If I wasn't the star performer in every course or extracurricular activity, I always feared I'd go back to being perceived as the black sheep. In time, I equated acceptance based on my achievements as love. On the other hand, if I failed at anything, then I felt devastated and assumed I was unlovable.

Because I was overworking myself to prove to others that I was worthy, I ended up exhausted and burnt out. In the early stages of my career, I endured years of bullying from a male boss who was transparently jealous of my accomplishments. After dealing with the hell at work, I would return home to an unappreciative husband. I ended up having a breakdown. During this dark period of my life, I felt worthless, used, and taken for granted. I recall my husband telling me that I had to "suck it up" and deal with the bullying from my manager at work because I was the "breadwinner" of the family. If I lost my job, we would struggle not only with our finances but also with providing stability for our daughter. She was sick with an autoimmune disorder at the time and required frequent visits to the doctor. I felt the weight of so many responsibilities on my shoulders. I had nowhere to unload them or anyone to turn to for support.

Eventually, I knew my life had to change, even if it meant going through a terrible divorce. Those of you who have experienced divorce likely understand the roller coaster of feelings that come with such a difficult situation. While on that roller coaster ride, I learned so much about myself. I realized that there were parts of me that had not yet fully developed and that the hurt from my childhood had bled out into my marriage. I wanted to grow. I wanted to experience life differently. I was tired of feeling unloved, worthless, and defective. I visited a counselor to find healing and empowerment. These life events ignited a strong desire in me to help others through life's most painful moments, putting me on the path to becoming a counselor.

Through my training in psychology, hypnosis, and parts therapy, I unearthed the power of my own inner acceptance. I found inner acceptance after my divorce, and my goal is to help you find it before you face a devastating life event. Then when the unexpected happens, you can bounce back with the inner resilience you already possess. Chances are if you are reading this book, the devastation may be present or has already happened. That's ok! You can still access and apply the methods I'll teach you in this book. I used the very same skills that I will teach you in this book, and it will be as life-changing for you as it has been for me. Even if you've already experienced hardship in your life—and

I'm sure you have in some way, shape, or form—this book can still help you to get past it and move forward.

In this book, I will teach you how to transform what seems hopeless into an opportunity for joy. You'll learn how to feel connected to all your experiences. You will develop a strategy to transform your inner critic into one who advocates for you and believes in you. You will learn how to embrace your innermost thoughts, even those you've labeled as "bad," by shifting your perspective to show that you are in control of them. After all, you're the only person who can hear your inner thoughts anyways!

From this new perspective, you'll experience regulated states of consciousness; that is, you'll be the one in charge of your thoughts and reactions to the world. You will notice an improvement in your internal dialogue, keeping yourself from getting stuck mentally or acting out in ways that you later regret. With the new perspective that comes with true inner acceptance, you will see the world and your place in it with fresh eyes.

Once you have learned these skills, you will naturally begin to take better care of yourself. If you follow the directions in this book, you will receive outstanding results in your life; from breaking free of your past to replacing negative thinking patterns with positive ones. By applying the knowledge inside this book, you will learn incredible truths about yourself and be able to accept yourself as you are and who you know you can become.

Inner Acceptance

Inner acceptance is the ongoing process of welcoming all your parts and seeing them as having positive intentions for you, even when those parts seem to cause more harm than good (Schwartz & Sweezy, 2020). It is common to judge parts of us that are flawed and unwanted, so we tend to lock them away. When you lock them away, you rob those parts of the freedom to become healthy versions of themselves. But when they are locked away, they do whatever they can to get out. When they do, those locked-up parts burst out of you like a raging tiger, leaving you to deal with the carnage left behind. This book suggests that all of your parts are welcome. You just need to learn how to repair your relationship with the parts in your mind.

Life will fall into place the way it is meant to. You can't change the future by overthinking things. What you can do, though, is gain a new understanding of your inner mind and embrace it to change your life.

In the following chapters, I will teach you how your parts have developed over time with your life experiences and how they speak to you in your inner world. You will learn the power of your unconscious mind and how it interacts with your conscious behavior. You'll discover how to become curious about the different parts in your mind and gain the tools to satisfy that curiosity. You will learn how to embrace all parts of your inner mind and use them to overcome any situation you might face. By the end of this book, you will be more focused, present, and intentional because you'll know that you can create a change that is sustaining, even in difficult times. More importantly, you are going to feel fantastic about yourself and walk away with an action plan to start applying what you have learned immediately.

Reading this book will not solve all of your problems, but it may illuminate them in a way that allows you to look at yourself and your life differently. I am thrilled that you have chosen to embark on this journey. Imagine having the ability to heal your inner wounds without relying on medications or other crutches for the rest of your life. You are in control much more than you believe. Now, let's get to work and breakthrough these limiting patterns and get you on the path to living the life you want to live.

Chapter 1:
How Inner Parts Develop

To be fully functional, each human being needs to express freely the five basic powers that constitute human strength. These are the power to perceive, to think and interpret, to emote, to choose, want (desire) and love, and to take risks through the use of imagination.
—John Bradshaw

"I feel so utterly devastated and lost," said a client of mine—let's call her Lisa—who found herself shutting down and withdrawing when she perceived her boss was hyper-critical of her work performance. Even if the feedback was balanced and constructive, she could not help but feel inadequate and upset. As a result, she felt she was walking on eggshells whenever she was at work. But, this feeling eventually followed her away from the workplace, and she became more and more quiet and withdrawn. The more she shut down, the more she internalized her feelings of inadequacy, which affected her relationship at home and, perhaps ironically, her performance at work. Anytime she received criticism at work or home, Lisa told herself she was not "good enough." She felt trapped and hopeless, and as these thoughts compounded, her inner mind experienced serious harm.

Lisa struggled with something that all of us deal with at some point in our lives—she based her self-worth on how she thought others saw her. To feel accepted and valued, she felt she had to impress her peers, so she began playing the role of a perfectionist. While this pushed Lisa to get better and be better at her job, deep down, she felt fake. She found the constant need to exceed people's expectations very overwhelming. Seeking that constant approval was a daunting task for Lisa, and she played that perfectionist role for many years. By the time she realized what was happening, she was overworked and dead tired.

Together, we explored her history, connecting moments from her past to her present experiences. She recalled her parents shaming her if she did not receive perfect grades in her courses. "If I didn't get an A," she said, "it meant I didn't try hard enough, and only failures get below an A on their assignments." Lisa reported that she never felt like she could ever measure up to their expectations. These feelings were very similar to the ones she felt when her boss criticized her work.

Inner Acceptance

At some point in your life, you have probably felt like Lisa—as though no matter what you do or say, you'll never meet someone else's expectations. Lisa's perfectionist part was attempting to protect the most vulnerable part of herself—the pain of feeling rejected and inadequate. But you don't have to be stuck feeling that way. Diving into Lisa's history enabled her to see how old feelings from the past had attached to her present-day experiences, providing her a new lens that helped her better understand her story and the activity going on inside her mind. She realized the perfectionist part was a role that formed to protect her vulnerabilities, and she could help it to find a new role.

From this, she learned how to accept all parts of herself. Her thoughts slowly transformed as she internalized her revelations, which ultimately changed her behavior. Lisa reframed her core beliefs about herself, which you will learn in later chapters, and was honest about her vulnerabilities of rejection and inadequacy. By owning them, she nurtured autonomy, self-confidence, compassion, and profound inner wisdom that ultimately changed her life. You can change yours too.

We are born with different parts inside us that evolve and shape over time as we have experiences. Many scholars on this topic will tell you your childhood still exists within you and affects how you think and feel in your adulthood. In this chapter, you will gain insight into how your innermost thoughts develop over time, allowing you to have the same kind of self-understanding that helped Lisa change her life for the better.

Let's start from the beginning. Every child has parents or caretakers, and we first form our opinions of ourselves through our experiences and interactions with them. If you behaved according to their wishes, you were considered good, and if you didn't, you were bad. We learn how to continually seek approval from others because being a good child helps you feel loved and accepted on the inside. A child internalizes the messages based on the input received from significant people around them. You may find out that you fear rejection or disapproval from others now because you have been conditioned since childhood to seek approval. When you don't get that approval, chances are you feel vulnerable, just like Lisa. Rejection hurts and creates anxiety when the goal of every action is to please someone else.

In childhood, your parts are in their early stages of development. Jean Piaget's theory of cognitive development highlights the "little scientist" early stages of childhood development. As kids grow and interact with the world around them, they perform experiments, observe and build on ideas and information.

When faced with difficulties from the age of 2 and up, you had to interpret and adapt to situations. The success of your adaptation, however, always depended on whether the adaptation warranted praise or punishment from your parents or other authority figures. We internalize situations of praise or punishment based on how we reacted to them rather than the experience themselves (Woititz, 1983). Anytime you found yourself feeling utterly embarrassed, shamed, shut down, or overwhelmed as a child, a role or behavioral part developed as a response. But, being in the early stages of

Inner Acceptance

its development, this role you've adopted is only an "immature" part of who you are. If that part doesn't develop further and stays stuck in the past with its childlike nature, it may contribute to certain unfavorable behaviors and outcomes in your adulthood.

You may have had a wonderful childhood and formed a close and strong bond with your parents, or you may not have had the best upbringing. Whatever the case, those early relationships helped shape your behavior today. Many parents, completely from a place of love and support for their child, never allow their child to encounter any sort of disappointment, which sometimes means they don't teach about the bad behavior or decision-making. For example, I had a client who found it difficult to hold down a job because she frequently called in sick. This tendency developed early on when her mother allowed her to call out of school when she didn't feel like going. The absence of accountability robbed her of learning how to handle difficult situations. She learned how to cope by taking the easy way out—to quit. After she quit her job, it was further proof in her mind that she was damaged. The cycle had to be broken.

If you're interested in learning more about how seemingly positive parenting strategies can backfire in the long term, consider reading *The Coddling of the American Mind: How Good Intentions and Bad Ideas Are Setting Up a Generation for Failure* by Greg Lukianoff and Jonathan Haidt.

All that said, your childhood isn't a crystal ball that tells you what your future will be. Case in point, I've had several clients who had wonderful childhood experiences yet suffer significantly from anxiety or depression. When your childhood doesn't have the answer, you can look to instances of pain experienced during adolescence or young adulthood for the answers. For example, if you were involved in sports and you felt your peers outperformed you, it may have been easy to internalize the agony of your inability to impress your parents or friends. Perhaps, you were bullied for no reason in the hallways in high school. The list goes on.

But sometimes, memories of your past may seem a little fuzzy. We do not always remember things exactly as they happened because emotions get involved, inviting us to make sense of the past through their lens. In that way, perceptions of a past event may be a mixture of fact and fantasy (Hunter, 2005). When we recall a memory, we actually recall a memory of an emotional memory that isn't particularly accurate (Nongard & Woods, 2018). It's kind of like playing the game Telephone, and the message has totally changed by the end of the game. Our brains are fragile and are not as accurate as we like to believe them to be.

Nonetheless, what you think and believe to be true determines how you feel and how you behave. According to Bradshaw (1996), our degree of happiness and self-satisfaction depends on getting our basic needs met. He states that our emotions are energy in motion, and if you are out of touch with your feelings, they become repressed. Your energy has to go somewhere. Either you end up having an emotional outburst, or you implode, which is why the concept of inner acceptance and releasing these pent-up emotions is critical to your emotional freedom.

Inner Acceptance

Over time, as we continue to be exposed to these situations in life, we develop a belief system about ourselves and others. According to Backus and Chapian (2000), emotional discomfort (emotional pain) never killed anyone; however, our misbeliefs tell us that emotional discomfort is terrible, awful, wretched, and horrible. When in fact, although not a lot of fun, it can be endurable.

All of our emotions and needs, whether good or bad, need to be validated to establish inner balance. By only accepting the good parts of yourself, you implicitly reject the bad parts, and they eventually go to work behind the scenes and start becoming a power of their own. Ever found yourself blowing up on someone without warning and then think, "Wow, I'm out of control." It is because the stored energy of the rejected part has to release itself somehow. So it comes out full blast, and then you're left wondering, "What the hell did I just do?" From this, a cycle of guilt and shame is set in motion.

I like to use the example of a teapot. You put it on the stove, and then it screeches loudly when the water is just hot enough. Now, imagine your brain being like a teapot. As the water ("bad" emotions) boils, the vent and water gap are filled with steam. When there is too much pressure in the teapot (your brain), the gas will force itself out of the vent without warning, just like anger, anxiety, or sadness. When we allow our anger, fears, or despair to become repressed, the pressure builds up and eventually needs to come out. And it will always find a way out, often at the most inconvenient times! Ever sat on the couch watching television and then suddenly get hit with a surge of anxiety? Have you ever been on the verge of having a panic attack for no apparent reason? This happens because the anxiousness needs to escape somehow. After all, there's simply no additional space in your brain to hold it in.

I had a client, Susan, who came to therapy because of an issue with her father. "He is making me feel responsible for his inability to take care of himself," she said, "and I feel so guilty when I enable him." Susan shared that her father would convince her of his helplessness and guilt and shame her until she gave him money to gamble or drink away. As a child, Susan's parents instilled in her the belief that she should always help others regardless of whether she wanted to or not. She felt responsible for the happiness of others.

This belief system worked for her as a child but not as an adult. A part of Susan always knew that her dad was taking advantage of her. Yet, she continued to enable him because of her belief from childhood. "It makes me so angry and confused when I tell him I can't help him because I feel like I'm obligated to. I get so aggravated that I end up blowing up on my husband, and he doesn't deserve that." Susan internalized a significant amount of guilt because she felt required to help her father. She felt like a bad person when she could not help him, so she repressed those feelings and kept giving in to his requests. Over time, the hidden anger had to force its way out, and it came out like a beast toward her husband. The cycle of guilt, shame, and anger continued.

Perhaps, there have been times in your life when you blew up on someone out of anger and then felt ashamed afterward. The teapot metaphor resonated with Susan,

Inner Acceptance

and it can serve as a vital reminder to stick with the inner work I discuss later. When Susan realized she was a boiling-over teapot, she found the courage to begin the process of reframing her beliefs and establishing new boundaries with her father. Ultimately releasing her guilt and shame. She discovered not only that some of her beliefs were limiting or caused her pain, but that she could create new, helpful ones. Her relationship with her husband improved. Her father learned to respect her boundaries, and her life completely changed. Once she was set free from a faulty belief and gained inner acceptance, her anger subsided tremendously. By the end of this book, you'll have the tools to do the same for your own pent-up emotions.

Let's go back to your childhood for a moment, to get a better understanding of how the parts of you develop over time. Emotional wounds stemming from a negative experience or even actual trauma or abuse, result in the creation of different parts designed to help you adapt to those situations. But those parts were immature, and to make sure you behaved correctly, you both consciously and unconsciously looked to your parents and other authority figures to approve your new behavior. Over time, you may have found yourself striving for their approval or pushing parts of you aside to become the person your parents wanted you to be. This kind of approval helps us feel loved and accepted. The absence of that love and acceptance breeds feelings of worthlessness and contempt.

Some children even experience physiological issues such as headaches, fatigue, inability to relax, or upset stomachs that carry over to adulthood. As an adult, those physiological effects either get better or worse, but so do other issues such as loneliness, anxiety, depression, relationship problems, or other behavioral problems. These are problems that many people experience every day. Once you learn where they come from and how to deal with them, you will experience life differently.

For example, suppose a parent verbally punishes their 4-year-old child. Over time, the child may find themselves withdrawing and becoming quiet to show obedience to their parents. As this person grows into an adult, they may find it challenging to get feedback, criticism, or demands from their manager, or others, because they perceive the manager as an authority figure, much like their parent was in their past. They will use the same coping mechanisms they used when they were 4 years old; withdrawing and becoming quiet. Over time, this behavior becomes a part of their personality. They end up shutting their true self down and then work diligently to be a false person seeking approval from others. Deep down, they feel like a fraud, defective and inadequate.

As adults, we carry the memory of the wounds and hurtful experiences of how others reacted to us negatively in our past. Based on how we interpreted or internalized these situations in our history, we misinterpret our vulnerabilities. Some of these vulnerabilities may have been shame, unmet needs, loneliness, or a feeling of being unimportant, unloved, or a failure. Because we experienced these vulnerabilities, to protect us from feeling that awful experience ever again, particular parts develop into protector roles—childlike protectors. Ever gotten so angry at someone that you realized you acted like a total child when you

Inner Acceptance

reflected back on that situation? Happens all the time! This is why.

The protectors that you developed jump in and try to protect potential violations to your vulnerability and think they are protecting you from getting hurt again. Most of the time, though, your protectors have been trapped in your unconscious mind and are the same as they were when you were a child, meaning they have little to offer when confronting adult problems.

You may see a protector role come out as raging anger or a visceral desire to withdraw from others (Emmerson, 2003). These parts become defensive coping mechanisms that lay dormant until something triggers them to become active. Our unconscious mind contains all these deeply embedded parts. There, they maintain their own memory and communicate with each other forming a sort of defense-mechanism coalition (Holmes, 2007). Now, you might be thinking that it's like multiple personality disorder or something. But no, this is not pathological in any way. In fact, it is natural and healthy to have various parts.

Accepting the idea that you have various parts that are doing the best they can to protect you and help you handle situations is life-changing. Learning the genesis of your beliefs and parts is the precursor to finding true inner acceptance. Interestingly, some studies state that when you recall your history, what the mind cannot remember, it will create. You will never truly see things today from the vantage point of yesterday. However, what we do recall best is how those experiences made us feel. Recognize this quote? "I've learned that people will forget what you said, people will forget what you did, but people will never forget how you made them feel" by Maya Angelou. Our feelings dictate what we end up remembering about situations. We remember them by the filter we've used to perceive it.

Another client—I'll call her Kara—had an extreme form of anxiety related to completing assignments. "Every time I get an assignment at school, I feel this surge of fear and uncertainty that overwhelms me so much that I freeze and just want to run away and get out of the room." The anxious part of her that she described just wanted to escape what seemed like an overwhelming situation. When I asked her whether she could recall times in her past where she felt the same way, she immediately spoke about her mother. She described her mother as a good mother but very stern and hard. Kara felt like she could never live up to her mother's expectations. Even when Kara earned perfect scores on her assignments, she never received praise from her mother.

Much like the other patients I've described, Kara was always seeking approval from a parent (her mother), and she tied her self-worth to her mother's reactions to her. When she did not receive the approval she desired, she would internalize the disappointment. Because of the disappointment she felt deep within her, she freaked out whenever there were assignments to complete. At times, she questioned herself in her mind by thinking, "I'm such a disappointment, why even bother?". Kara was living with a constant feeling of never being good enough, which hurt her so profoundly that the prospect of facing that disappointment again led to extreme anxiety. Kara had seen four other therapists before

Inner Acceptance

seeing me. It was very challenging for her to recall specific situations in her past that attributed to her feeling inadequate and disappointed in herself. Still, she remembered the voice in her head telling her, "Escape! Get out." Perhaps, there are times when you feel that you aren't good enough, no matter what you do. Luckily, there are ways out of this mental trap.

In therapy, Kara learned the origin of the disappointed part of herself. Realizing that it presented itself as anxiety (her protection from pain), she gained a new awareness about herself. She saw how the disappointed part was still carrying the wounds from her childhood experiences. She realized that this disappointed part of her was overworked and holding on to old feelings that no longer made sense in her adult life, preventing her from living the life she wanted to live.

I coached Kara through a series of steps on how to comfort and release the deep-seated pain and disappointment of her childhood. She immediately felt calmer, focused, and more compassionate toward herself. In time, she turned the disappointed part of her into a tool for resilience. She changed the belief that she was full of inadequacies and defects to that of a strong woman capable of doing great things with pride and courage. This switch was truly life-changing for Kara, and you can experience the pure acceptance of your inner mind as well.

You might be saying, "How do I accept a part that I hate so much?" I totally get that. My question to you is, have you ever tried listening to it, or do you just block it and push it away? When you block it and push it away, how can it learn to trust you and start working differently for you? How do you feel when you are shoved to the side and left unheard? That part of you that you are pushing away feels the same way. The next chapter will explain these things in more detail.

Chapter 2:
Your Inner World

*The power to change truly lies within the client,
rather than in the therapist.*
—Roy Hunter

Have you ever experienced a time when you were faced with a similar, if not the exact situation, and you responded in two different ways? When facing a familiar situation, you may suddenly notice that something is different from the last time you had that experience because you're approaching it with a different attitude, logic, or emotion. You may also find yourself wrapped up so tightly in your thoughts that you become confused or think you've gone crazy. These are all normal feeling states—we all wear different hats for different occasions—but this can distract us from fully experiencing the inner acceptance of our minds.

Our inner parts like to contradict each other. Have you ever found your parts locked in a tug-of-war—one part bent on pulling you full speed ahead toward something and another that's so overwhelmed it sits down to keep you from moving forward? Have you ever found yourself thinking something so random, so unlike your usual self, that you begin to believe that you are an irrational and unworthy person deep down? Maybe you have parts in your mind that make you feel confident, happy, and loving, and yet other parts deep down judge you, telling you that you aren't good enough or that you are a "bad" person.

As we continue to build the habit of labeling ourselves as good or bad throughout our various life experiences, what we think becomes our reality. Our brain becomes hardwired and conditioned to think in a specific way and with a particular filter. The human brain is designed to find and detect patterns. We use those patterns to look for danger, spot food, and make predictions about what we think will happen (Vance, 2016). These patterns condition our brains into experiencing and expecting things in our lives in certain and definite ways. Our life experiences consist of memories, both bright and good, and dark and bad. Almost always, we choose to lock the bad ones away and do everything possible not to experience problems and difficulties in life. How can you truly measure which parts of life are good, if you never allow yourself the chance to experience the bad ones?

Inner Acceptance

All experiences shape who you are. Learning to accept all of them as contributing, in some way and varying degrees to the greater whole, is a fundamental concept as explained in this example: Imagine looking at pond water in a microscope. You'll see parts of the pond water with various microorganisms and other unique properties. But all of those parts combined create the magnificent droplet of water that you see as a whole, away from the microscope. The parts of you are just like pond water.

If you discard the elements you've labeled as "bad," it is nearly impossible to accept the greater whole of yourself. All parts are welcome in your inner system, whether you agree with them or not. Even your "extreme" parts have a rationale for their behavior. They feel driven to perform to the extreme because of certain beliefs, emotions, and energies that entered your inner world from trauma, family, life experiences, or society. These extreme parts become your personal burdens (Schwartz & Sweezy, 2020), causing you to believe that you are worthless, not good enough, unlovable, etc. Therefore, you end up behaving in specific, undesirable ways. Because you carry these burdens, you have protectors that work really hard to get you to avoid feeling that awful pain. These protectors come in the form of anger, sadness, or fear.

All protector parts have the positive intention of keeping you from experiencing the pain of your wounds or vulnerabilities carried by your inner child part., even though what you tend to notice more is their self-destructive tendencies. In general terms, anger gives you the energy to protect yourself. Fear gives you the energy to run away from things perceived as harmful or dangerous. Sadness gives you the energy to become self-critical. These protector parts tend to keep your subpersonality parts, described below, hidden most of the time.

I purposefully began this book by describing the inner-child part because it is the most critical of true inner acceptance. As mentioned before, you may have had an excellent upbringing and childhood, but the inner-child parts of you still carry wounds. But, you see, other parts of you can be wounded as well. How those wounds manifest and are dealt with play a key role in the inner dialogue you experience every day. To help us have a foundation for understanding this inner dialogue, let's talk about your different inner parts and see how they impact your life.

There are several different types of parts, each with its own story, motivation, strategy, and behavior. Some of them are similar and share the characteristics of each other.

- Inner-Child Part
- Happy Part
- Anger Part
- Sad Part
- Helper Part
- People-Pleaser Part
- Failure Part
- Perfectionist Part
- Comic Part
- Fearful Part
- Intellectual Part
- Exhausted Part
- Healer Part
- Pain-Stopper Part
- Guilt-Tripper Part
- No-Emotions-Allowed Part
- Creative Parts

Inner-Child Part

The inner-child part often feels abandoned and unheard and experiences shame. Sometimes, this part will shut down or withdraw from others to hide. When triggered, it also feels unloved, unworthy, depressed, scared, and shy. Sometimes, this part causes you to stay in relationships for far longer than is healthy. This part may cause you to hoard unnecessary items because it cannot let go of perceived sentimental value. It may even make you feel lonely or that you don't belong.

Your inner-child part carries your wounds from various experiences, which are later activated in your adulthood. Because of your inner child, there may be times when you find yourself playing emotional games with people and manipulate them to get your needs met, maybe because you find it difficult to be straightforward and assert yourself.

After all, your inner child part does not know how to communicate effectively in some instances, so it can use deception and trickery to fulfill its desires. There may even be some overindulged aspects of yourself that make demands of others and feel irritated when others do not respond to your needs. With this kind of entitlement, you may expect others to meet your needs and then blame them for your unhappiness when they don't. You may feel needy and look to others to take care of you, or sometimes, you don't know what you want and become indecisive and dependent. You may look at your past and wish you could rewrite it, and you fantasize about the future, but never live in the "now."

Happy Part

The happy part experiences excitement, joy, and pleasure. Your happy part basks in a good mood and experiences lightheartedness, curiosity, fun, and autonomy. It adds a positive flair to your mood and helps you feel good. It enables you to be content in most situations and projects an uplifting spirit to those you encounter. This part may cause you to feel euphoric, and it boosts the good chemicals (serotonin and dopamine) in your brain. You may find yourself talking and connecting more when your happy parts are activated. When you experience happiness from this part, it helps your body to have more balanced sleep and avoid insomnia. When activated, this part wants you to take care of your body by eating healthy food, exercising, and enjoying vitality in life.

Anger Part

The anger part can be authoritarian and often hates other parts of your internal system. For example, the angry part may hate your submissive inner-child part. It becomes frustrated very quickly and can rage like a storm to keep others from hurting the wounds it's protecting. When activated, it can cause you to act stubborn and pessimistic—in addition to unleashing your inner warrior or rebellious roles. This part wants you to stand up for yourself or uses aggressive influence to ward off threats. You may find yourself exploding at times. These outbursts will be more profound when you experience shame, fear, or embarrassment. This part may even attack you at times, telling you that you shouldn't exist.

Sad Part

The sad part may cause you to perceive yourself as defective and never feel satisfied. Sometimes, you may feel empty inside and move from one experience to another, trying to find satisfaction but without luck. You may feel hopeless and frozen in despair when this part is active, causing you to feel deeply saddened by the world around you. You might also get stuck in the sadness, unable to say or do anything except wallow. Grief and loss often activate the sad part. Sometimes, this part undermines your self-confidence and self-esteem, telling you that you are worthless and can never amount to anything. The sad part tricks you into thinking that you're alone and no one will be interested in you. It tricks you into thinking that no one will ever like you.

Helper Part

The helper part provides comfort and nurturing to your life and others. It can be a very healthy and positive part. Still, it's easy to overindulge in this area, especially if you lose yourself because you constantly help others and put their needs before your own. When activated, the helper part can cause you to feel compassion towards yourself and others. The helper part also helps your internal parts when they are in conflict with each other. Your helper part allows you to feel good inside when you're conducting charitable acts towards others. It helps you to be patient and kind.

People-Pleaser Part

The people-pleaser part avoids conflicts, accommodates often, always agrees with others and is deeply hurt when you perceive someone is upset with you. You may find yourself continually trying to please people and win their love, but no matter what you do, it is never enough. You may find that you walk on eggshells around others because you are afraid of rejection or criticism. This part may make you feel like you must fit into a certain mold and will shame you when you don't fit in. There also may be times when you give so much to others that they feel entitled to it, leading you to feel taken advantage of. If this part dominates, it's easy to feel like a victim if the help you give others is not reciprocated. In other words, you may find yourself doing everything you can to make someone happy, but if they become unhappy with you, you might turn things around and make them think they did something wrong.

Failure Part

The failure part causes you to feel inadequate and tells you, "You are not good enough." It often waits for something negative to happen or expects worst-case scenarios. It has already predicted your failure and wants to protect you from that pain by encouraging you to retreat instead of going for it. How does it protect? By encouraging you to withdraw and not put yourself out there. When your failure part is activated, you might be sensitive to rejection. However, this part may push you to work harder out of a fear of failure, though it may motivate you by calling you lazy or stupid. This part can cause you to become stuck in the "analysis paralysis" because of the intense fear of failure.

Perfectionist Part

The perfectionist part is your inner critic and is obsessive about your appearance and how others perceive you. It has similar tendencies to the people-pleaser part. It pushes you to be the best, look the best, and act the best. This part has very high standards and wants you to be popular, credible, professional, and worthy of the highest awards. This part always needs a plan—it hates uncertainty, loves control and ties self-worth to external things such as your title at work or other people's opinions about you. There may be times you find yourself worrying obsessively about the opinions of others. You may pay attention to every single detail and repeat things over and over in your head. If this part does not experience the approval that it wants, it often feels defeated. Even if you did well on a task, the perfectionist part tells you it still wasn't good enough.

Comic Part

The comic part also wants to be liked, but it uses humor to hide deep levels of sadness or fear. There may be times when you are overly sarcastic or making fun of yourself in front of others to appear happy and fun, but deep down, you are protecting your emotions. Although laughter is an essential element in life and can have valuable benefits, if the comic part is activated to protect a wound, it can intensify sadness through jokes that hit a little too close to home.

Fearful Part

The fearful part doesn't deal with uncertainty well, so it causes you to feel nervous. It creates stories and jumps to conclusions, even if the narrative is totally off the wall. Often, it is overly worried and overthinks everything. Other times, it is excessively skeptical and unwilling to take risks, always imagining the worst-case scenario. Above all, the fearful part prefers consistency and certainty. It is on the hunt for danger and will activate the fight-or-flight system in your brain if anything feels amiss. It will put up walls to protect you, making it difficult for you to trust others, and yet still, you may feel frightened most of the time, panicking easily. At times, the fearful part and the failure part overlap in many ways.

Intellectual Part

The intellectual part of you helps you to know everything! It figures things out and uses resources to make decisions. It thinks through all available facts and evidence. It can access all of its knowledge within the unconscious and bring that understanding to the surface. It helps you to accomplish your tasks by prioritizing, organizing, and reminding you of what needs to be done. This part can assist with helping your other inner parts to rationalize and thinking logically together in certain instances.

Exhausted Part

The exhausted part just wants a pill to feel better because it's so overworked. It wants a quick fix, lacks patience, and feels bad about itself. You may determine the only way to experience happiness is through a mind-altering substance, or you become addicted to activities that distract you from your feelings or thoughts. You may feel numb at times. This part is desperate to find relief and may experience overwhelm.

Healer Part

The healer part is wise, grateful, curious, calm, comforting, and compassionate. It always has access to words of wisdom to help you feel connected to something greater than yourself. Some people refer to this healer part as God, higher power, or inner strength. When activated, this part helps you to feel at peace. It helps you feel surrounded by protection, comfort and inner strength. This part is also referred to as your wise self or wise mind, which you will learn more about in Chapter 7.

Pain-Stopper Part

The pain-stopper part will binge, cut, threaten suicide, and resort to drugs or alcohol to avoid experiencing pain or vulnerabilities. This part is unsure how to handle the inner turmoil in your mind. It assumes there are no options for you to experience relief except by acting out physically. In most cases, when this part causes someone to cut, for example, that person will experience a sense of relief. Typically, these folks cannot verbalize what they are feeling or assert themselves in any way, so they cut to get their frustrations out. For those who resort to substances, the substances enable them to escape the pain, so they don't have to feel the inner pain and discomfort from whatever it is going on in their mind.

For those who are suicidal, it is because the pain-stopper part just wants to stop the pain as quickly as possible. It often does not want to die. It wants to stop the inner pain and feels it has no other choice. If you or someone you know is suicidal, please obtain professional help or go to www.suicidepreventionlifeline.org.

Guilt-Tripper Part

The guilt-tripper part feels responsible for everyone's problems and readily takes on blame, even if it is unearned. This part often forms a connection with the people-pleaser and the perfectionist part. It can cause you to feel like you'll never be able to forgive yourself and often struggles when outcomes or situations turn out negatively. It longs for comfort and attention from others. You may feel deprived of your individuality and cannot pursue your interests, so you become resentful. Because your thoughts become resentful, you later experience guilt and shame for those thoughts. There may be times when this part will shame you if you're impulsive or engage in an indulgent behavior. You may find that you attack yourself by taking, or not taking, specific actions. Anytime you feel that you "should" have done something, your guilt-tripper part is active.

Emotions-Not-Allowed Part

This part requires you to shut down because you were shamed if you ever expressed or talked about your feelings. It expects you to read people's minds and to know things, even though you were never taught how. This part often feels overwhelmed by your emotions because it can't make sense of them. It has an even harder time communicating those emotions to others. It's wary of other people's emotions too, becoming confused or intimidated by others showing strong emotions.

Creative Parts

Your creative, intuitive, and imaginative parts help you to solve your problems. You may find, at times, that you can think outside the box and come up with fantastic solutions you feel good about. When you tap into your creativity and imagination, new possibilities form in your mind, enabling you to see different perspectives, find hope, and discover ways of resolving your inner conflicts. You can consider your creative parts to be like little professors, curious and full of wonder. These parts are always working for us, and we must activate them more often.

Many other parts are not listed here, and not all of them are equal in their function. You will notice how some of these parts share the same elements of different roles and act out in similar ways. Some of these parts may have received a lot of attention from you, while others were shunned and hidden away.

No matter how out in the open they are or not, our parts talk to and interact with each other. Have you ever found yourself saying, "A part of me wants to eat that slice of cake, but then there is another part of me that says I'm a pig and will get fat"? What about these: "A part of me wants to lash out at him/her for being so stupid, but another part of me tells me to stay calm and open-minded" or "A part of me knows that I need to make a decision, but another part of me doesn't want to take the risk"? Chances are, you occasionally find yourself stuck as your parts battle it out in your mind because they're trying to help you all at once.

With so many parts vying for your attention, you may also find that you react differently to the same situation. For example, imagine you have been missing out on social activities and want to go out and have fun. Your friends call you up and ask you to hang out and you run right out the door. A few days later, they call you to go out again and you tell them you're sick, or you make up an excuse because you suddenly have a fear of being socially awkward. If all of your parts do not feel "in the mood" at the time, they can go back and forth between various feeling states. For example, the guilt-tripper part may cause you to feel guilty for not hanging out with your friends and spending time with others.

Or your fearful part may be afraid of being criticized by your friends if you were to act distant or strange because you were feeling socially awkward that day. The people-pleaser part might be telling you that if you don't go, everyone will abandon you and you'll end up alone forever. And so on.

The next time you find your different parts going back and forth in your mind, try to stop and notice what is happening. Which parts are doing the talking? At the heart of all these inner parts and roles we play are emotions, and they are central to how we interpret situations and frame the stories we tell ourselves about our lives. Listen to the story going on in your mind as you continue to read this book. Try and notice which

Inner Acceptance

parts of you are jumping out for attention. Which parts of you relate to what you're reading, and why? To resolve your inner conflicts, start now by being curious about what goes on in your mind and how it causes you to behave. Later, I'll teach you to validate parts of you, so they become less polarized or stuck, and you can move forward with a decision that you will not later regret.

I once had a client, who I'll call Brooke, and she came to therapy because she was struggling with weight loss and self-esteem issues. "I feel so fat and ugly. I feel gross inside, and even if my husband tells me I'm beautiful, I don't believe him." In her youth, she was a very athletic cheerleader and gymnast. After giving birth to her first child, Brooke struggled to drop the baby weight. She began to believe that she was unattractive and put the brakes on her sex life with her husband. Luckily, her husband was very understanding. He gave her the space she needed without forcing anything or making her feel guilty about their lack of sex.

However, because Brooke felt fat and ugly, she began to pick her skin. Because she felt imperfect and gross on the inside, her unconscious adopted the behavior of mindlessly picking her face to shore up that belief. When she had a bump on her face, she would pick at it until she got all of the perceived bad stuff out of it, and then experienced relief when she felt she was getting rid of the imperfections. She also recognized an inner dialogue between her parts when offered snacks or desserts from coworkers: "A part of me knows that I should say no and I know what I need to do to lose weight, and the other part of me says, 'Take the damn cake,' and the other part of me feels gross after I eat it." Brooke had multiple layers of parts that caused her to behave in undesirable ways, and she thought it was all too much to bear.

We worked on these parts individually and healed them by learning to hear their sides of the story and allowing them to negotiate with each other. Brooke learned how to be curious about why those parts were conflicted. She learned how to appreciate them for trying to protect her in some way, even if she didn't agree with them. She found inner acceptance for all of her parts and learned how to love herself from the inside. She learned to not label her parts as good or bad, but to see them as part of her with positive intentions. Through the healing journey of inner acceptance, she stopped picking her skin, felt better about her weight, and naturally started taking care of herself. In terms of her sex life, she became more spontaneous with her husband, and she started enjoying sex again. Her mind was no longer blocking her from experiencing life with joy.

The benefit of understanding your inner world is the gift of feeling normal and included. Feeling normal and included helps you to realize that you are not some lonely person isolated on an island with this crazy enigma of a problem. You learn how to accept yourself, quirks and all. You learn how to look at your different parts and find ways to be compassionate and curious about yourself. The more you uncover about your inner world, the more you build a foundation of knowledge about yourself, which eventually turns into inner acceptance and self-love.

Inner Acceptance

You can have a dialogue in your mind and be completely normal! People tend to think that inner dialogue with parts is pathological, but it is healthy to have the exchange. In fact, you learn more about the way you think and why you make decisions the way you do. Parts help you learn to appreciate your incredible mind and its ability to problem-solve and be creative. You just have to give yourself a chance to listen to the dialogue unfold. Listening without judgment is the very first step in this process. Now, it's time to learn other methods to add to this one.

Chapter 3:
The Unconscious Mind

*The infinite intelligence of my subconscious mind
reveals to me my true place in life.*
—Joseph Murphy

"I felt that damn blanket!" exclaimed Andrew as he discussed his experience in hypnosis. Andrew had been struggling with a mild form of autism, obsessive thoughts, and anxiety for most of his life. These issues left him in a state of hopelessness and confusion after he endured a major surgery on his spine. Andrew was frightened of the possibility of injuring himself after the major surgery. Every small movement he made intensified his fear of damaging his spine. He

Inner Acceptance

was terrified of having to return to surgery, or even worse, end up in a wheelchair for the rest of his life.

Andrew decided to come to see me because he was desperate to control his anxiety. It was preventing him from getting a job, causing havoc in his relationships, and creating a life where he barely wanted to get out of the house. As an extremely talented drummer in a local band, his hopes and dreams playing the drums diminished quickly before his eyes. He was fearful of returning to play the drums, which ultimately caused him a significant amount of sadness and discomfort.

The goal was for Andrew to find comfort so he would not feel nervous all the time. In traditional talk therapy, it was difficult for him to put words together or even describe how he felt. Because he was unable to put his emotions into words by talking about them, it further deepened his frustration and anger toward himself. Unable to use words to describe his feelings, he lived his life experiencing feelings through images and sensations. If he wanted to describe an emotion, he would refer to a song or lyrics to offer examples of what he was feeling inside. Music was his connection to his emotions. Drumming was his outlet.

In his hypnosis session, I guided him through imagery and breathing patterns that induced a state of relaxation. To achieve his desired emotional state, he would play his song of choice lightly in the background as he listened to my voice. Andrew had a part of him that would constantly make him feel nervous and frightened over everything. He had obsessive thoughts that would repeatedly play in his mind, and what he longed for was for this part to relax. This is where the suggestion for a blanket came into play.

During the hypnosis session, I suggested that Andrew imagine being surrounded by a blanket of comfort. I described the blanket in detail for him, allowing his imagination to create the effect for him in his unconscious mind. Andrew imagined a nice warm blanket surrounding him, protecting and comforting him. As he experienced the blanket's comfort, I suggested to him that he could use this blanket as the tool that was there for him whenever he needed it. All he had to do when he felt his anxiety rising was to close his eyes, take a few deep breaths, and imagine the warm blanket surrounding him. Every time he imagines that blanket covering him and offering him comfort, he can find a state of calm. Free of anxiety with each additional breath.

After his first session, Andrew went home to test out the blanket experience for himself. We call this self-hypnosis. For a week, Andrew practiced using the warm blanket in his mind during specific times of the day. The first thing when he woke up during the day, he would practice self-hypnosis. Anytime he felt anxiety bubbling up within him, he'd practice. And every night before he went to bed.

When he returned to therapy the following week, he reported his anxiety was minimal and he was living life as if he never had anxiety. He was thrilled. Finally, he had a tool that made sense to him. Because he experienced his world through sensations and images, hypnosis worked wonderfully for him. It was a powerful experience for him, and he discovered that he could have control of his inner experiences. Andrew felt like a completely new person. He experienced a level of autonomy and freedom from his anxiety. After a few weeks, he realized that he didn't have to practice self-hypnosis as often or multiple times throughout the day. Day by day, his brain was rewiring, and he was feeling great.

Eventually, Andrew learned that he could start his day with the warm blanket self-hypnosis, which was enough to carry him through his life. He is focused, calm, and in complete control. Obviously, some days are better than others, and he still needs to do a little tune-up every now and then. However, today, he reports that he has better relationships, he landed a job playing the drums, and is finally back to living life again! This story highlights the fantastic benefits of hypnosis and the power of your unconscious mind.

The unconscious mind has many responsibilities. There is a physical aspect where it controls and regulates functions within our bodies, such as breathing or our heartbeat. These things happen naturally and involuntarily. You don't have to think about your heart beating. It just beats. You don't have to think about blinking. You just blink. All of these things happen unconsciously. There are also elements of the unconscious mind that impact our behavior. You react to things without even thinking. You just act. You can, however, teach your unconscious mind to learn positive new responses versus knee-jerk reactions to things.

After receiving my Master's degree in counseling, I spent time as an intern, learning how to apply the skills I learned in grad school. Most schools teach the typical counseling methods, such as assessing clients, developing treatment plans, and how to diagnose mental health disorders. However, if you want training in a specific treatment area, like Cognitive Behavioral Therapy, you must study those things on your own. My supervisor, Dr. Marty Lerman, is a psychologist and a clinical hypnotherapist. I know, I know—you're probably thinking, Oh God, here we go, another voodoo person. But just hear me out! When I discovered Doc Marty (as he prefers to be called) was a hypnotherapist, my mind went haywire. *He must be into witchcraft*, I thought. *He is playing with the devil.* My skepticism was primarily based on my experience in the Southern Baptist community. So I prayed about it. I prayed for God to close the door in my face if what I was about to walk through was not His will for me.

Well, that door stayed open. I learned so much about the unconscious mind that aligned with my spiritual beliefs that it was too difficult for me to walk away. I saw rapid—and I really mean *rapid*—change in front of my eyes from clients who were experiencing profound turmoil. Hypnosis transformed their lives. They were living again, breathing again—hopeful and joyous. I wanted to dig my heels in further and see how I could help transform lives too.

Doc Marty was a hypnosis instructor, so he encouraged me to consider becoming certified, and I did. I doubted my ability to successfully apply hypnosis into sessions with my clients due to various inner critic reasons, yet I

Inner Acceptance

continued to push through. Doc Marty and I held weekly supervision meetings as part of my required clinical hours for the state board of practitioners. In these meetings, we discussed the treatment plans for my clients, including the therapeutic techniques I planned on using during those sessions. Doc Marty encouraged me to use Roy Hunter's "Parts Therapy," which is a specialized hypnotherapy technique. I spent a great deal of time studying and researching these techniques and similar courses like "Internal Family Systems Therapy" by Richard Schwartz.

Through this experience, I learned more about how our unconscious contains inner states or parts that maintain their own memory and often communicate. Memories and emotions that are too painful, embarrassing, shameful, or distressing to face are stored in the enormous reservoir that makes up the unconscious mind, shaping our choices and emotions. The information inside the unconscious impacts our inner parts and how they play into our thoughts and behavior. As I began practicing these techniques, I often encountered the fearful part of my clients; afraid of reliving a terrible experience that their protector parts have worked so hard to lock away. I found myself reassuring clients that this type of work aims to take those memories and release them from their inner system. Once they've found healing in the releasing and letting go process, their protector parts relax as well.

Our imagination, creativity, and intuition are also found in our unconscious. The unconscious mind wants to do whatever it takes to feel good, even if it develops an immature way of doing so. Think of your unconscious as continually working to help you avoid encountering anything unfavorable or undesirable because of your actions. Importantly, however, your conscious mind is what makes those judgments about what is unfavorable or undesirable. It's the rationalizing part of you that tries to make sense of the world, while the unconscious is where those judgments and rationalizations are stored. This disconnect between the conscious and unconscious mind is one of the reasons why hypnosis is so effective.

Put simply, hypnosis bypasses the critical evaluations of the conscious mind and gets straight to the unconscious part, activating it. To bypass your mind's critical conscious element (your inner critic), a hypnotist must work to get your mind and body into a relaxed state. The hypnotist offers images or sensations for you to imagine in your mind, and then your unconscious is activated. Once the unconscious part of your mind is activated, any suggestions made to it by the hypnotist are accepted as reality and considered favorable, bypassing the conscious mind's judgments.

But what does this all mean? Allow me to give you a quick example. Have you ever woken from a dream and thought the dream actually happened? When the brain is sleepy, any images taking place at that time are what the brain accepts as reality. This is exactly what hypnotism aims to mimic, which is why it can be so rapid and effective at creating behavioral changes. When a hypnotist suggests that you imagine something while you are sleepy, your brain yields to and accepts this reality state. When the brain begins accepting new thoughts, images, suggestions, and solutions, it will create a new neuropathway in your brain. This "rewiring" of the brain takes advantage of the brain's neuroplasticity—its ability to physically change as we adopt new ideas, habits, and mindsets. Because of neuroplasticity, you can literally change your thoughts and your brain!

If you want rapid change in your life, hypnosis may be the key to unlocking your potential. Speaking with a qualified hypnotherapist or hypnotist is essential before deciding to undergo this sort of treatment. I encourage you to talk with someone that has been certified in a program offered by the International Certification Board of Clinical Hypnosis or the Ericksonian Institute. Why? Because their training was completed over time instead of a fly-by-night weekend course. There are other reputable clinical hypnosis certification groups, but I highly recommend these two.

Hypnosis can provide you with the tools you need to create a sense of relaxation and comfort in your daily life. Our brains need periods of rest to function at optimal levels. Hypnosis provides an effective, safe way to reduce stress and create that time for rest. For hypnosis to work for you, you must believe and expect that it will help you. When your mind starts thinking optimistically and you experience a state of calm in the hypnotic state, there is no denying that it will work for you. I'll discuss more regarding expectations in Chapter 9.

Psychologists and scientists are still trying to learn more about the unconscious mind. Current theories suggest the unconscious is like a reservoir, storing all of your memories and emotions. The unconscious wants you to feel good. When you have painful experiences, the unconscious tries to bury the memories and emotions associated with that pain deep to protect you from re-experiencing that pain. When the unconscious is ready to resolve the repressed memories, it can do so, but it would not risk the chance of harming or overwhelming you. Your unconscious mind also plays a huge role in the childlike parts that we discussed in earlier chapters. Although the childlike roles that become a part of us do not seem logical or helpful at times, your unconscious designed them for self-preservation.

I had a client, Lilly, who came to therapy because she had struggled with depression after having an abortion in secret as a teenager. "I'm a murderer," she said. "I make bad choices, and I am an embarrassment to myself and my family. I shouldn't be alive." Lilly internalized grief and shame to the point where she did not want to live anymore because she did not think she was deserving of love. She had experienced this pain for over 30 years. It was embedded in her. No matter how many attempts she made at self-forgiveness, she never truly forgave herself because she didn't believe that she could.

Lilly and I worked through inner acceptance of her parts. We validated and accepted the part of her that felt unworthy, and we listened to its story. We allowed that part of her to provide images of moments in her life where she felt undeserving of love. Lilly exchanged silent inner dialogue with these parts. Eventually, she released the burdens of those stories by casting them into the light. After she released the pain, she described feeling as if she were empty inside, like a shell. She indicated the underserving part had been with her for so long that she now didn't know what the new role for that part could even be.

Inner Acceptance

This moment was where we called upon her higher power or inner strength to impart words of wisdom to help the part that was healing. We asked for guidance on how to embrace new qualities now that she had released her pain. Then the words of wisdom started rolling in. Lilly's higher power gave her the understanding she needed, and she committed to living by it. Her life had changed. Still, to this day, Lilly tells me that she often goes back to that safe place in her mind, and she calls on her higher power in times of distress, feeling amazing every single time.

Hypnosis has become far more accepted in the medical and psychology professions. There are a multitude of studies from Europe that validate its effectiveness from a clinical perspective. There are many misconceptions about hypnosis, and unfortunately, it has become a source of fear and entertainment in the United States. For one, it is not mind control.

"Nothing has any power over you until you give it power over you." I'm not sure who coined this phrase, but there is so much truth in those words. Repeat that sentence a few times and see how you feel after. It's quite liberating. You have the potential to be in charge and in control of your mental state far more than you realize. Hypnosis offers the solution to activate the self-energy you need to function and behave in healthy, positive ways. Once you realize that you can become the wise healing agent that you need your entire life, your life will change. This doesn't mean you don't need God. In fact, it's about connecting with the part of God that is already within you. All you have to do is call upon your higher power or inner strength— it is readily available.

Hypnosis allows you to experience freedom from your negative experiences, and it takes advantage of the power within your unconscious mind. You do not need to cultivate it. It is already there. Healing, strength, and guidance are accessible, like fruit from a tree—plentiful and within reach. You will not experience any negative or unwanted emotion or behavior through hypnosis unless you willfully invite it.

Do you have to do a hypnosis session to achieve these results? No, but hypnosis is a beautiful way of learning how to enable self-healing, which I discuss in the next chapter. The answers already lie within you. The key is learning how to process and release your emotions, and although you can do much of this yourself, the guidance of a counselor or hypnotherapist can provide meaningful support on your journey. You can release hurtful experiences, repair your self-image, and learn how to accept uncertainty by living fully in the present moment. By reading this book, you're already taking the leap of faith into a new chapter of your life.

Chapter 4:
Opening the Door of Your Mind

> *The unconscious mind always operates in the present tense, and when a memory is buried in the unconscious, the unconscious preserves it as an ongoing act of abuse in the present of the unconscious mind. The cost of repressing a memory is that the mind does not know the abuse ended.*
> —Renee Fredrickson

A cornerstone of my counseling practice is to use mindfulness-based techniques that help clients experience relaxation and activate the parts of their minds enabling the healing of emotional issues. It doesn't sound very easy, but it's effortless, and I'll walk you through some mindfulness steps here shortly. But first, let's talk about what mindfulness is and how it can help heal inner pain.

Mindfulness has much in common with transcendental meditation (TM) and hypnosis as well, despite looking somewhat different. A mindfulness activity might only take you about 2 to 5 minutes to complete. In comparison, transcendental meditation is recommended to last 20 minutes, twice a day and requires specialized training from a yogi master.

I've personally experienced transcendental meditation, and it is quite a beautiful experience. There are several locations throughout the world with certified trainers to teach their preferred way of meditating. I encountered a problem with TM because I found it difficult to set aside time to practice meditating before breakfast or before dinner. As a working mom of four children, it can be challenging to find the perfect time to meditate. However, when I meditate using this technique, it is very peaceful and I notice that I'm a more regulated mom emotionally.

Hypnosis can be completed alone or with a trained clinician. Sessions usually take 45 to 90 minutes or longer, once or twice a week. However, all three of these techniques require you to close your eyes to achieve a relaxed state, making them slightly different from my preferred intervention: using the waking-trance method. The waking-trance method is very similar to mindfulness and you only need about 2-5 minutes to complete the exercise when feeling anxious, sad, or angry. For inner

Inner Acceptance

wounds that are far more traumatic, it can take a clinician 45 to 90 minutes to assist.

The waking trance phenomenon is the ability to have your eyes open while in a rested state. Not sure that this is possible? Well, have you ever daydreamed? Your eyes were wide awake, your mind was fully engaged with an image or idea, but chances are you found yourself recharged afterward. A waking trance is like a daydream, and you enter that state more often than you think. Ever watched a movie and found yourself crying with the character or jumping out of your seat during a scary scene? It's not like you were in the scary movie, but the terror felt real. You could imagine it was happening to you. That is your waking-state trance phenomenon. Once you begin to imagine it, see it and experience it, you've tapped into your unconscious mind.

The benefit of the waking-state phenomenon is that you can remain awake and still reap the amazing benefits of the experience of the trance effect. Some of my colleagues may argue here that the client needs to be in a full hypnotic state at the deepest level for healing to be long-lasting. Still, in my experience, I've found that the waking trance is just as impactful. The majority of my patients take what they've learned and applied it for themselves in their own homes. By staying awake and aware, they are not reliant on me, the therapist, for their long-term success. When they do return to therapy, it is either for a quick "tune-up," or they've encountered something else in their life that they need help with. With this in mind, let's look more deeply at the waking-state phenomenon and how you can take advantage of mindfulness practices.

Mindfulness Meditation

Here is a mindfulness meditation to try on your own. This meditation is typically used when you're experiencing a bout of anxiousness, sadness, or anger in a particular situation. I've called it the Three-Step Restart Technique. You can also find a guided meditation at www.inneracceptance.com, where you can listen to a recording that walks you through the process

Most of my clients prefer to close their eyes for this meditation, but some clients choose to gaze at an object or the floor. The most important part of the Three-Step Restart Technique is the simple sequence you'll follow:

1. Find it.
2. Feel it.
3. Free it.

Step 1: Find it. Take three deep, cleansing breaths, and after the third breath, close your eyes. Return your breath to its normal pattern. Allow yourself to feel the sensations all over your body, see the different images in your mind, and listen to your thoughts as you breathe in and out. Find the most prominent sensation, image, or thought. You will know what it is because you will experience heaviness somewhere on your body.

Step 2: Feel it. Feel where this prominent thought, image, or sensation is inside your body. Notice where it shows up. Perhaps, you feel the heaviness or sensations in your head, throat, neck, shoulders, stomach, or chest. Allow yourself to feel the sensation without judgment.

Inner Acceptance

Feel the sensations that accompany the thought or image you're focusing on.

Step 3: Free it. Extend gratitude to the part that is showing up by thanking it for trying to help you in some way, even if you don't understand or agree with it. Ask that part to relax just a little so you can begin to focus on the present moment. Let that part know that you realize it is overworked in this specific situation. Still, you do not need to act 100% from this emotion at this time, because acting 100% out of the negative emotion will block you. However, if you can observe this emotion as being a part of the experience, there is no need to act fully in the emotion. It now has permission to relax. Next, become fully aware of the present moment, noticing your sitting position, the smell of the air, the sounds around you, and the new lightness of your now-relaxed body. Then, open your eyes and feel entirely focused on the world around you and the tasks in front of you.

Focusing on your breath in Step 1 sets the stage for the rest of the process. When we bring more oxygen into our bodies and release toxins, it helps us release tension and relaxes our minds and bodies. We often do not give our bodies enough periods of rest throughout the day, but this simple act of breathing ensures that we do. When you proactively give your brain moments of rest, you are helping it recharge and refocus. Just like a computer, when your brain starts getting glitchy and frozen, you simply restart it, and voila, it usually starts working just fine again. Purposefully controlling and focusing on your breath allows you to recharge your brain, which ultimately helps your mind and body perform at optimal levels.

As you progress in Step 1 and return to your natural breathing, you practice mindfulness by going inside yourself and noticing the sensations, thoughts and emotions that are happening within you in the present moment. The simple acts of noticing these sensations and feeling them are the opposite of blocking them out and pushing them away. You can validate them as real and present in your life without judgment. Your teapot is not building pressure when you purposefully sit with those feelings and allow them to be for the moment.

The second step is feeling those sensations with intention, allowing just enough time for them to be processed without making you feel overwhelmed. In fact, this will make you feel more relaxed! In this step, you must notice where you feel the physical sensations on your body. You are building a relationship with yourself and learning more about the way your body responds to things so that what you're experiencing or sensing no longer seem foreign to you. You'll learn to know exactly what is going on in your mind and body when the physical sensation arises, and you'll know exactly how to resolve the inner conflict when it surfaces.

A core concept of this kind of self-care is treating each part of you as if it were a friend inside of you. Validating and accepting each part's perspective, i.e. the sensations they create, is extremely important because when you block or shun them, they only become resentful, as any friend would. When your friends are hurting or angry, do you tell them to shut up and go away, or do you allow

Inner Acceptance

them the chance to be seen and heard? When you tell someone to shut up, how do they respond to you? What if you say, "Tell me more, I want to help you"? In the latter instance, chances are your friend is visibly lighter and ready to share with you.

The final step is to release unwanted sensations and relax. When you pinpoint the heaviness of an undesirable feeling in your body, you can imagine each breath relaxing that part more and more. You can imagine the unwanted feeling flowing down a stream or floating away in a balloon. The process of letting go enables the active parts to relax, and you can regain your focus and control of the situation you're facing.

Keep in mind that you can use this skill when you are feeling great as well. When you experience joy, you can use the Three-Step Restart Technique to learn how to savor that joy and feel the effects of its warmth on your body. Feeling these emotions on your body helps you to feel alive and fully present in the moment. Anytime I take a walk outside, I use this technique. I'll notice the leaves on the trees. The smell of the air. The sounds of the birds, or the laughter of children around. I'll pay attention and observe nature. This exercise offers you a sense of peace and belonging within yourself and the world around you.

If you find that it is difficult to address your unwanted emotions at a particular time or place, set an intention to come back to it later in the day. Set a reminder on your phone to remind you that you have an appointment with yourself. And if right now a part of you is telling you that this is a silly idea, that's the part that wants to reject ideas.

Just laugh with it a little and say hello. Let that part of you know that it wants to be critical, but it can step to the side because you need to focus on this task for yourself, so you can start making life changes.

Practicing this technique first thing when you wake up every morning is an excellent way to start your day. You may tell me that your mornings are chaotic and that you don't have time to do this. I totally get that. But, you have to use the bathroom at some point in the morning, right? I know it sounds weird, but set a timer on your phone for 2 minutes, use the restroom, then sit there for 2 minutes, and work through your Three-Step Restart Technique. I've even had clients use the technique while brushing their teeth, making their morning coffee, etc. You have 2 minutes to spare. Just find the time to do it, and start your day with it.

I also encourage you to use this technique throughout the day when you feel sensations surging through your body. Maybe you get an email from a coworker that rubs you the wrong way, or maybe your spouse said something that made you angry. No matter what happens, when you feel those unwanted sensations rising, take a time-out and go somewhere. Go back to the restroom, if that's the only place you can go, or to the breakroom or your car. Go somewhere for 2 minutes and practice the technique. I promise no one will criticize you, because 2 minutes is not excessive—and your mind will feel better. You'll feel happier, more present, more focused and ready to take on the rest of the day.

Inner Acceptance

When it seems like everything that could go wrong is going wrong in your day, I recommend you to use this technique at night before you go to bed as well. Thirty minutes before you lie down, grab a piece of paper and write down all of your tasks and worries. Then, set the intention that you will permit yourself to get rest for the evening. That way, you can focus on your list tomorrow. Then, apply the Three-Step Restart Technique before you lie down. If you incorporate one or two of these ideas, you will notice a difference in how you feel. You will find that you are less on edge at home and at work, and you'll clear out the inner conflicts that distract you from being productive.

Going Beyond the Critic

Perhaps, there are times when your inner critic jumps in and tells you that you aren't doing enough and compares you to others or keeps you stuck in the past or worried about your future. When you notice this happening to you, stop and smell the roses. In other words, notice that your inner critic is active. Validate it by acknowledging it and saying, "I see you, I hear you, and I feel you." then, start paying attention to the world around you. Notice the details of the room you are in. Use your five senses and notice the beauty in the details around you.

Several of my clients, who are parents, criticize themselves for not doing enough with their children because they are occupied with work or chores around the house. If you find yourself criticizing yourself this way and notice you are stuck in the past or worried about the future, stop what you are doing and go to your children and be present with them. Feel the texture of their hair in your fingers. Notice the warmth of their smiles and their glowing nature. Give them a nice hug and embrace the power of the unconditional connection you have with them. Get involved with what they are doing. Teens, on the other hand, would rather you leave them alone. However, there is a way to get involved in their world. Ask them about their favorite music or games. Get them to share a story with you that is important to them, even if you don't identify with it. This simple act of taking 10 minutes to be present with your children, discredits any of those criticizing thoughts that enter your mind and help you be mindful of your present moment.

The Three-Step Restart Technique is instrumental in accessing acceptance, which is explained more in the next chapter. Before beginning the next phase of acceptance, I need you to be open-minded and in a relaxed state. If you find that it's too scary to talk to your unwanted inner parts or you think doing so may trigger an adverse reaction, do not proceed further. However, after reading the next chapter, you may find that it is possible to test out inner acceptance for yourself, with the promise that if it starts feeling too difficult, you will go at a slower pace or seek help from a therapist.

Chapter 5:
Accessing Acceptance

When something is accepted for what it is, it no longer has power. It is then just something experienced rather than something I hate, or I fight, or I'm restricted or obsessed with.
—Richard Nongard

Would you behave differently if you discovered your inner parts, all of them, have positive intentions for you? I believe that once you learn and believe that all of your parts are trying you help you, you no longer need to fight or overcome them. You don't have to get rid of them or push them away. Instead, you can discover more about what each part is trying to do for you and attempt to make a positive connection with it. You can offer all of your parts appreciation for their efforts and compassion, so they begin to trust you. These parts are simply scared, in most cases, about what would happen to you if they didn't do their job.

Critics may argue otherwise, claiming that some parts drive people to do terrible things. But acceptance does not mean we have to endorse or condone what those parts want. It simply means accepting the thought, feeling, sensation, or moment for what it is. This means having an inner dialogue with these parts to find out their stories. Once we understand why a part is causing us to behave or act in a certain way, then we can act with compassion towards it. Compassion towards yourself and compassion towards your inner parts balances your system and enables you to find freedom from judgment and tension.

Showing compassion towards a part means letting it know that you understand why it is doing what it is doing and then teaching that part how to find a new, healthier role for you. When we try to get rid of parts, even negative ones, they do not go away. They lie dormant and end up blending with other parts, possibly sabotaging them. Keeping an open mind, you must find acceptance and compassion toward these unwanted parts and help them repair the relationship within your inner mind to learn to trust you as an adult and adopt a new role.

I had a client—I'll call him Bob—who came to therapy because he was deeply suicidal. "There's this huge part of me that wants to commit suicide, but I don't want to die. I just want to get rid of the pain." Bob knew the

Inner Acceptance

inner turmoil and conflict inside him caused him to have suicidal thoughts to escape the pain. So many people have suicidal thoughts, yet they truly don't want to die. They can no longer bear the pain. That suicidal part of Bob, which he later named Sid, thought that suicide was the only way to remove the pain. Sid did not realize that there were other options to consider and experiment with to lessen the pain's burden.

Bob engaged in an inner dialogue with Sid by accepting that part of him, even though it was doing more harm than good, and learned how to remove judgment from Sid so he could hear Sid's story. Sid shared that anytime Bob got happy, someone hurt him, so Sid shut Bob down and made him feel empty inside to avoid the potential pain that someone he loves might hurt him. When Bob finally heard and understood what Sid was doing and why he learned how to extend compassion towards Sid. He realized that Sid was working hard to protect him from experiencing heartbreak, which changed the way Bob viewed Sid. Bob understood why Sid was working so hard to protect him, and by extending compassion, Sid's intensity lightened.

Through further exploration and inner dialogue, I taught Bob how to reassure Sid that he didn't have to work so hard anymore and that he could find a new role for Sid that didn't require him to shut Bob down when he was feeling happy. He practiced the Three-Step Restart Technique and proved to Sid that there could be happiness and that it is safe to feel joy. Soon enough, Sid trusted Bob. The relationship within Bob was repaired. He gained inner awareness, inner acceptance and understanding that enabled him to live a life free of suicidal thoughts—a life where happiness could exist without the fear of the threat of emotional pain.

I chose to highlight this story in particular because suicide is a very sensitive topic in our society. You may even have found that you can't talk about suicide, especially in certain circles, and the desire for repressing your innermost thoughts increases. I hope that in reading this story, you feel a new sense of hope. Whatever the case is, being open, accepting, and compassionate towards all of your parts enables them to evolve and adopt more positive roles once they feel heard and understood. You may find there are parts in your mind that you label as scary, intrusive, or odd. You may find that your past attempts to hide them and lock them away always ends with them finding a way of sneaking around and catching you off guard. Hopefully not, but you may find that you're better off locking them away because you think there is no hope in helping them. If some of your parts are too difficult for you to accept, speak with a counselor. They can help you process them.

RISE Up

Learning how to accept all of your parts may seem like quite a challenging task, and rightfully so—it is not meant to be easy. But how can you experience the wholeness of your life if you continue to lock your parts away? Typically, the part you lock away is your inner-child part, and another part of you tries hard to protect the wounded piece of it. By understanding your wounded inner child's story and motivation, you can begin to work with it. The goal is to get into a relaxed state of mind and activate your imagination so you can

Inner Acceptance

successfully have an inner dialogue with the locked-away part.

Here are a few ways I help my clients to gain acceptance of their parts. I call it the RISE Technique, and you can use this in conjunction with the Three-Step Restart Technique.

> **R**—Request your critical parts to step aside so you can become curious about your locked-away part and focus on it. Assure the exiled part that it's safe to share its story, and ask all parts to allow inner dialogue to take place.
>
> **I**—Invite the part to a safe place where it can share its story and speak to you directly.
>
> **S**—Show compassion toward the part as it's sharing the story with you and listen to the story.
>
> **E**—Extend gratitude towards the part for working so hard for you all these years.

Request. Requesting your non-exiled parts to step aside is crucial because you do not want other parts to judge or be fearful of the unwanted part. It also ensures that the unwanted part can trust you when you say it is safe. Without the other parts in the way, the unwanted part will open up to you completely because it knows there will be no judgment. To ensure this happens, promise all of your parts that you will not relive your painful trauma again, no matter what gets shared.

Invite. You are creating a safe place, completely removed from the places where the painful events happened, and you will be safe to share whatever needs to be shared there. In this step, you invite the unwanted part to this safe place. Begin by imagining what that part looks like. Learn about how old that part is by asking it. Picturing what this inner-child part of you looks like is important because you will activate your imagination and walk with the inner child to that safe place. I've had several clients whose inner-child parts find solace and safety in places like playgrounds or parks, near lakes or waterfalls, or at a safe place from their childhoods. The goal is to find a space where the part can share openly but not relive the pain.

Show. The unwanted part needs compassion as it's sharing its story with you. Offer it. At times, you may find that the exiled part will share images or memories that were painful, and it is OK to feel that pain. It lets that part know that you get it. For example, the inner-child part is often still stuck in the past because it had no one to count on for comfort and help when it needed it the most. Typically, this step is where my clients find a way to provide the support and comfort for that part the way it needed before. They will report holding the child or rocking the child, wiping away tears, or hugging and holding them. In this stage, you become the healing agent that you needed all along, providing comfort to your inner child, so it no longer carries the painful burden of having no one there for them.

After providing comfort to the inner child and allowing the full story to unfold about everything it's been holding onto, ask that inner part of you if it would like to let go

Inner Acceptance

of those old memories. Letting go of the old memories will offer a sense of relief and freedom. Here, most of my clients will get creative, casting those old memories into the light, putting them on a rocket ship and blasting it away, filling up balloons and watching them float away, or burning them in a fire. There are so many options where you can be creative and let those images go.

Extend. The final step is to extend gratitude to the exiled part for the release of those inner wounds. As you do this and watch those last images disappear, you may notice that it is easier to breathe. Perhaps, you feel just slightly lighter than before, but intuitively you know other layers need to be released at some point. Set the intention that you will get to know and understand those parts of you as well, and have the expectation that you can go to this safe place anytime you want and enjoy the process of letting go.

This exercise may be difficult for you to experience when simply reading the information. I've added an audio version of the RISE meditation on the website www.inneracceptance.com. The audio version of this technique can be very healing for you. It may take you a few times to listen to it before your parts open up. What is critical here is that you set the intention that you will not fight or try to get rid of the parts. You simply want to be curious about it and help it to heal.

To be curious about your inner parts, you must learn how to communicate with them. Inner dialogue with your parts needs to come from a place of curiosity and willingness to help. At times, it is normal to have your critical part step in and attempt to cast a shadow on the undesired part. However, you can simply ask that judgmental part to step to the side. This is a very important step because, for you to really understand the exiled parts of you and their protectors, you must come from a place of love and sincerity. Otherwise, the judgment will keep the part locked away.

Most of my clients report feeling a sense of freedom with the RISE technique because their inner wound was finally brought to light. They can sit with that part of them and provide the necessary comfort that they wished they had when the event took place.

I had a client—I'll call her Abby—who came to counseling because of the difficulties she had with codependency with her husband and her children. Codependency, for Abby, meant that she constantly used her people-pleaser part and sacrificed her personal needs to meet theirs. "They've all become so entitled that they won't lift a finger around the house to help me, and they just don't seem to care," she explained. She started to feel as if her life didn't matter to them, and she felt used and taken advantage of.

Abby internalized everything from low self-esteem to perfectionism and control issues. She was facing a downward spiral and needed help. I spent time teaching her how to set boundaries with her family, but the feeling of her inadequacy did not change. There was more to the story. Abby spent her entire childhood in an emotionally abusive situation with her step-father. He was in the military and was very strict on her. Abby reported her step-father was jealous of the affection she would receive from her mother and that intensified his anger and disdain for her. She shared stories of how he mentally abused her and made her feel like scum. Desperately wanting his approval to avoid being mistreated, she developed a people-pleasing role. This role helped her to be the quiet and obedient stepdaughter, and that role carried her through her adulthood.

Abby reported she fell into bad relationship after bad relationship when she grew older. She fell in love with men who she thought she could "fix" and help. That turned out to be a terrible idea, and the men she fell in love with would end up abusing her too. Feeling as if she was repeating the cycle of abuse, she went to church and met a man there that she fell madly in love with. Although she mentioned their relationship was much better than her prior relationships, deep down, there was the sense of not being good enough for him, so she would people-please.

To heal from the old pain of the past, we used the RISE technique in session. Using her imagination, her inner child took Abby to her grandparents' house by the lake. Together they cast the old memories of the abusive stepfather into the lake. As her inner child completed the healing process, she observed that part of her dancing with joy with the new found freedom of letting go of the past. When Abby watched her inner child dancing in freedom, she immediately started talking about all of the new qualities she wanted to manifest in life.

Abby reported that her life changed afterward. Anytime she felt insecure or codependent, she reminded herself of the experience of casting the wounds of her past into the lake and how she felt doing it. Abby had a new and positive inner strength when she learned to let go of the old feelings and thoughts that no longer served her. She grew stronger in setting boundaries with her family and started doing things to take care of herself more.

Considering Abby had experienced several profound traumatic events in her past, she needed to seek counseling from a professional for her issues. There were complicated issues that required the appropriate time to process through. If you find that you are working through the RISE technique and more layers to yourself need attention, you should definitely seek a therapist to assist you.

The RISE technique is a very useful method to help you heal from your past. It is also a great technique to use when you find there are parts of you that require some extra attention, and you can access that safe place in your mind by using your imagination. My clients go to a safe place in their minds frequently. They know exactly where to go when they need additional healing or when old feelings start bubbling up again and they do not want to relapse.

This is not a "one and done" technique. It is something you will use often when you find healing needs to take place.

Chapter 6:
Creating Inner Dialogue

Eventually, you will see that the real cause of problems is not life itself. It's the commotion the mind makes about life that really causes problems.
—Michael A. Singer

Learning to have healthy inner dialogue is extremely important for emotional regulation, stress reduction and inner healing. When you learn how to talk to your inner parts, you become fully present with the reality of what's going on inside of you in each moment. And when you are fully present, you see the story playing out in your mind better, with your inner parts taking center stage.

When you listen well, you will understand what drives your parts to exhibit extreme behaviors (Barbera, 2016). Instead of trying to analyze your emotions, merely listening to what they have to say validates and shows you appreciate them. When you extend validation and appreciation for your inner parts, they relax. You're able to access more resources and experience calmness and, as I discuss in the next chapter, your wise self.

This chapter aims to help you explore what is going on in your inner world so you can unlock all that potential. The questions posed below will help you navigate an inner dialogue that helps you find meaning in your parts instead of trying to eliminate their behaviors. You can journal these questions if you like or record yourself asking these questions in your own voice. The most critical part of the dialogue is noticing when judging or fearful parts show up and ask the questions. Politely ask the quieter parts to step aside so you can focus on the most prominent part. It's like asking one of your children to be quiet and listen to what their other siblings say. The parts of your mind are like different people within a family system, and they should be treated as such. You can do this courteously, setting an example for your parts.

If you ask these questions and find no answers are coming to you, that is OK. Do not force it. There may be parts of you that are just not ready to share their stories yet and are working on building trust with you. You may find that once you extend compassion and gratitude to a part that wants to shut down. It may offer you images, thoughts, and sensations that alert you to the fact that it's ready to share its story with you.

Inner Acceptance

You may also find that asking these questions results in a completely random response, or you may see an image that does not fit with what you were expecting. That's OK too. Many of my clients have expected a certain story from their past to surface, only to find a completely different one related to the emotional turmoil. Either way, go with it. Go with what comes to mind, and that story will unfold and reveal important truths.

Beginning a Conversation

Ask yourself these questions to begin the process of inner dialogue communication:

- In what situations do I tend to feel negative about myself?
- What words do I say to myself in those moments?
- What thoughts do I have in those moments?
- What's my attitude or behavior like in those moments?
- What do I look like in those moments?
- How does my body respond to those situations?
- What vulnerability is that part trying to protect me from?
- What is it trying to accomplish, for me, by judging or shaming me?
- What is its biggest fear if it didn't do this job for me?
- Can I ask this part to step to the side for a moment, so I don't feel overwhelmed by it?

If the part doesn't want to step aside, ask it why. Then, respond to the part and let it know that you will be able to focus better once it steps aside because you want to listen to it, and you promise nothing bad will happen. Once it steps aside, notice how you feel now that you have a little bit of space from it. If there is any judgment about that part, let it go. You want to feel curious about it, accepting and compassionate.

See whether you can extend compassion toward the part by letting it know that you understand where it's coming from. Then, notice how it responds to you. You may notice the activated part is calming down. Whatever the response, follow up by asking that part the following questions:

- What do you want me to know about you? Why did you start taking on this role for me?
- Do I have permission to heal the wound you have been protecting me from for so long, as long as I promise not to overwhelm you?
- Would you be willing to relax a little so I can help you to find a new role?
- Would you like to not feel that way anymore?
- Are you willing to separate for a bit from the part that is protecting you so I can take you to a safe place where you can share your story with me?
- Ask the part to share the story that it holds onto and the pain it feels in response to the attacks from the unwanted inner parts. Then, reflect on that story by answering the following questions:
- What happened in your childhood or during those experiences that caused you to feel that way?

- What are some of the negative beliefs you've built about yourself?
- Where do you carry those burdens in your body?
- In what situations are you carrying those old feelings and attaching them to your current situation?
- Is your inner child ready to let go of those wounds? Ask it.
- What positive qualities does that part want to take on in its new role?
- How can my wise self help me to take on these new qualities?

Earlier, I had mentioned we would often go inside our minds with the expectation to hear a particular story, but end up hearing something different. I had a client, I'll call her Tanya, who came to therapy because of severe anxiety. The anxiety was affecting her at work while driving and with her new boyfriend. At first, Tanya shared a story about how her mother remarried when she was a teenager to a man she never met. Tanya recalled the new step-father being very disrespectful to her and pushing her away from her mother. She ended up leaving home at the age of 16, bouncing around from couch to couch, and eventually dropping out of school. She reported experiencing intense fear of not knowing where she could lay her head at night and if she would ever amount to anything.

Listening for Answers

Tanya described her anxiousness as stemming from the belief that she had no one she could count on. This belief made her extremely anxious to the point where she was terrified of driving her car. If she was ever in an accident, she believed no one would be there for her. Her fear only worsened when she started becoming more committed to her new boyfriend. When Tanya did the exercise of inner dialogue and listening to her inner child's story, she assumed that the story would be related to the feeling of abandonment that triggers her anxiousness. What we found, however, was related to her burgeoning relationship with her boyfriend.

Making this connection took time. Going inward, she assumed the anxiety stemmed from her relationship with her mother, but having that bias caused her to struggle to interpret what her part was saying. I then asked her, "Since this one part is not very comfortable sharing just yet, is there another part that might be willing to help provide an answer?" It was at this moment where Tanya replied, "I keep getting the word 'dad' in my head, and I don't know why."

I then had her thank that part for showing her the thought of her dad and advised her to inquire whether it would share more. The inner child shared a story of her being about 4 years old when her father vanished. She said she never really knew much about him but heard horror stories about him that always frightened her. From these stories, we learned she had developed a belief that men would hurt her and abandon her. Tanya connected this belief to the present and realized that because she was in a committed relationship, deep down, she feared her boyfriend would leave her at any moment, causing her severe anxiety. With this connection made, Tanya accepted the story by validating it, showed compassion toward it, and then released it. Tanya realized this old story did not have meaning in her current life, and it was preventing her from fully living in a loving relationship with her boyfriend.

Tanya learned how to listen to her inner story such that she could be fully present, rather than assuming she knew. When you find that you are stuck with a part of you that is not willing to give you details or share its's story, thank it for trying and let it know that you understand and respect why it is shutting down, then invite another part to speak on behalf of the other part. When you try to quiet your mind, you will notice that many parts try to jump in because they want attention too! Notice those parts and activate them when you need to. You will be amazed at how willing these parts are to share the story of what's really going on behind the scenes in your mind. They are very chatty! You can then open up your imagination and your curiosity to learn more.

You will find that there are times when you think you already know your story but really don't. Once you learn how to ask the right questions and listen to the story within your mind, you will find meaning and connection. When you begin to go inward and have an inner dialogue, remove any expectations of what you think the story might be. Be open to listening to whatever comes to your mind. Really listen to what the parts of you have to say, and then you will be able to make the connections necessary in your life.

The inner awareness, acceptance, and meaning that you unearth from the inner dialogue is powerful. You begin

Shannon Mosher

to learn to appreciate more things about yourself because you realize that you are much more multifaceted than you think. Be open to what is going on in your mind. Be open to learning more about the story and the history of why you act and feel the way you do. Accept what is going on and be fully present with yourself. When you do, you learn self-love and inner acceptance.

Inner Acceptance

Chapter 7:
Your Wise Self

Who is the one human being in your life who can always be there for you, at any moment, no matter what happens? Who is the one human being who can understand, validate, and empathize with your pain better than anyone else on the planet? Who is the one human being who can truly know just how much you are suffering? You are.
—Russ Harris

We long to feel significant and to know that our lives have meaning and worth. There may be times when you don't feel like you're enough or have what it takes to succeed. But we are all born with a wise part within us—a soul, higher power, inner power, source, inner strength, God, or higher self. No matter what you want to label it, the beauty is that you have it. It does not need to be cultivated because it is already there. You can activate your higher power or wise self anytime you need to, and it can be a valuable wellspring to nourish your sense of self-worth.

The concept of your wise self does not discredit your religious affiliations whatsoever. If you find yourself praying or meditating, you are calling on your wise self. For those of us who pray, we typically thank our higher power for protecting us and our families, ask for guidance, request healing from sickness, and so on. Activating your wise self is like praying, so it may come naturally to you. But no matter what you believe, the concept of the wise self complements spirituality rather than challenge it.

In the last part of the previous chapter, I had mentioned that once you release all of the wounds and the burdens from those old memories, you have to replace it with something else. There has to be a balance in your internal system. If you have nothing to replace the old feelings with, you'll have no new direction. Tapping into your wise self, however, can help guide you on a new path and find a long-lasting replacement for the negative behaviors.

In this chapter, I will discuss WISE, a technique that I use with my clients when they need to tap into their wise self. Wise stands for the following:

Inner Acceptance

W—Words of Wisdom

I—Insightful Understanding

S—Strengths-Based Acknowledgment

E—Expectations

By learning this technique, you can access your wise self when you need guidance in critical moments.

Getting Wise

Words of Wisdom. In the first step, you ask your wise self to impart words of wisdom to you and your inner-child part. Just remain calm and listen in this step. Quiet is key. When you don't try to think about it and just ask your higher power to impart these words upon you, you will intuitively to obtain a message. Ask yourself, "What would my wise self say to offer me comfort or guidance right now?" Perhaps, you may find your wise self telling you that you did the best you could and that everything is going to be just fine. The words of wisdom may end up being words that soothe you, and that's fine.

Your wise self is always available to send you comfort, love, and the wisdom to access greatness within you. All you need to do is imagine the warmth of healing and love in your mind. Your wise self may not have words, but it may bring you a sense of peace. Listen to your heart's compassion for yourself. You're doing the best you can do now, and you did the best you could do in your past. Even if you made mistakes or were dishonest, you can extend self-compassion and learn from them. Your wise self can help you to abandon self-blame and humbly honor and own your choices. Your wise self can help you look at what's going well in your life and the things you can be grateful for. You will know when you've accessed your wise self because you will feel calm and centered.

Insightful understanding. In the second step, the goal is to change your "if-then" thinking. A good example of if-then thinking is changing "If I fail at this project, then I'm a failure" to "If I apply my knowledge in this project, then I'm adding value regardless of whether I fail or succeed." You may have tons of self-limiting language in your self-talk. This is where your wise self can help you gain an insightful understanding of a new way of thinking and believing, which carries over into the third step.

Strengths-based acknowledgment. In this step, think back to the moments when you accomplished something great or felt appreciated, acknowledged, or truly seen. Remember the specific skills and talents you leveraged under challenging situations, or how you helped lift someone up and enabled them to accomplish something incredible. Hone in all of the wonderful strengths you have that have pushed you through some of the most challenging parts.

You were born with innate talents and strengths. Regardless of how you think your strengths compare to others', those strengths are yours and yours alone. Your wise self can help you recall all of your incredible strengths to help shape a positive mindset. This strengths-based understanding will help you take what you sucked at and turn it into something you are strong at. Your wise self can help you.

Inner Acceptance

Expectations. In this final step, you must change your expectations from the negative and believe that you will have an optimal outcome with your life goals. If you expect that you will suck, you will suck. If you expect that you will be awesome, you will be awesome. If you expect that you'll be resilient and become stronger when some things don't work out the way you hope, you will. Change your expectations with the help of your wise self. Know that even when life doesn't follow your ideal plan, you are capable of learning from the experience in some way. Yes, there may be some parts along the way that suck, but that does not mean you suck or you are doomed.

You have to evaluate where you put stock in your life continually. If you are struck with anxiety, what is it that you value more than your fears? This is a terrific question because it requires you to think of other possibilities than the fear-based mindset that keeps you stuck. Doing this kind of inner work isn't easy. Still, your wise self can help you to seek out alternative ways of viewing situations and help you to find peace and comfort in the discomfort.

Often, the source of our distress comes from looking outward rather than inward. Ask yourself what you measure yourself against. Who or what are you comparing yourself to and why? Is it beneficial for you to constantly feel inadequate and miserable because your life is not like someone else's? Create a new story for yourself with your wise self. Create a new perspective on how you see yourself and your strengths. Know and affirm that you have value, that you are worthy, and that you are genuinely accepted on the inside.

Sometimes, we do not realize how our beliefs and self-talk limit us. You may find yourself getting stuck, and maybe you're overthinking or not listening to your wise self because of the deeply embedded belief you have. I totally get that. When you are stuck, ask yourself, "How does thinking this way or acting this way move me toward my goals? How is thinking or acting this way moving me away from my goals or the outcomes that I want?" When you ask yourself these questions, it is important to validate whatever thoughts, feelings, or sensations arise, and then work toward an alternative solution.

You can find an alternate solution with your wise self once you learn to treat yourself with kindness. In other words, you want to deliver a message to yourself that is not harsh, critical, condemning, or judgmental. Your wise self helps you take action to remedy situations that are in alignment with the person you want to be. Your wise self can also set boundaries with your unwanted parts. It can tell the unwanted parts when their judgments are being destructive and encourage them to step aside, reminding them that although you're aware they want to help, their approach is not working for this situation.

Accepting Yourself in the World

Your wise self nurtures, loves, and guides you. Your wise self teaches you that you are accepted, trusted, worthy, and valuable. Your wise self reminds you of your resilience, strengths, accomplishments, and just how special you are. Your wise self tells you that you can do anything you set your mind to and that you are

Inner Acceptance

everything you've ever needed. You are enough. It also helps you to slow down and take things at a better pace. It can help you overcome any obstacle in your way and correct the course when you're in doubt.

Learning to accept outcomes when life does not go as intended is vital to making peace with your story in the world. Instead of beating yourself up about a setback, turn it around into something that you can learn from and bounce back from. Here are a few uplifting guidelines you could adopt to foster greater acceptance of yourself, even when life throws you a curveball:

- Accept yourself as you are. Period.
- Accept your imperfections. Period.
- Accept your vulnerabilities. Period.
- Accept your past as your past. Period.
- Accept the reality of your current situation. Period.
- Accept your discomfort and know it is sometimes unavoidable. Period.
- Accept that some things are uncertain. Period.
- Accept unmet expectations. Period.
- Accept self-compassion. Period.
- Accept self-doubt. Period.

If you work with these affirmation guidelines, you will find yourself creating personalized ones for yourself. You may find that you prefer to have your affirmations during prayer, or written on a Post-It note on your bathroom mirror, so you see it first thing in the morning. Whatever you do, make it a point to repeat your affirmations daily.

Each night before you go to bed, grab your journal and write down the things that went well for you. Cultivate a practice of identifying things that are positive and had meaning for you. Write down the gist of your self-talk throughout the day, and note any inner dialogue that you had with yourself to get through a challenging situation. Journaling is a very therapeutic method of reinforcing your progress and reflecting in times when you feel stuck again.

I also recommend writing down your goals in your journal. Try this prompt: "If you no longer experienced _____, how would your life be different? How would you feel? What thoughts or behaviors would no longer hinder you?"

There is power in journaling, and there are tons of gratitude journals out there to help prompt your thinking. I encourage you to get one! I plan on creating one soon, so be on the lookout for my upcoming book, "Gratitude Sprinkles."

To supplement your affirmations, you must learn how to reframe your negative self-talk into positive and helpful self-talk. Turning your self-limiting thoughts into thoughts that are more flexible and optimistic takes practice. In the next chapter, I will discuss how to reframe your self-talk into words of power in your life. Words that will move you and boost your motivation, rather than block and defeat you.

Chapter 8:
Reframing Your Thoughts

We're never going to debate whether or not your thoughts are true or false. What we're interested in is whether your thoughts are useful or helpful—whether they help you to live a better life.
—Russ Harris

We carry a significant amount of self-doubt, self-blame and guilt. We harbor various other negative thoughts about our inadequacies which destroy our self-confidence, self-esteem and motivation. We have cognitive biases and thought-processing errors that can lead us astray. Put all of these together, and you can see that the human brain likes to play the blame game and block out certain kinds of information to protect our self-esteem and guard us against failure.

Your negative thinking patterns are based on the psychological (not necessarily religious) belief system you developed when information was blocked in your mind. Beliefs are your assumptions of what you believe to be true, and they don't necessarily mirror reality. For example, you could have an automatic thought that says, "If I don't pass this test, it means I am stupid." Your belief system is activated, resulting in thoughts of I'm too unintelligent to master anything. So a vicious cycle of self-blaming and critical self-thought begins. If you think you are unintelligent and cannot master anything, imagine how defeated, depressed and insecure you would feel daily. Imagine what your body language or attitude would be like if you chose to believe that core belief on a daily basis. You'd feel miserable, inadequate and defective. You can see how quickly just one negative thought pattern can become a belief and ruin your day, your week, or even feel as if it has destroyed your entire life. That said, you do have the power to think differently.

Most sources say the five basic emotions are joy, sadness, fear, anger, and disgust. Understanding your emotions is crucial because they coexist with your automatic thoughts. For example, if you automatically tell yourself, "I'm unintelligent and mess everything up," chances are you are going to feel sad most of the time. When you feel sad, what happens? Typically, sad people withdraw from others. They stop doing pleasurable things and this leads them to feel like life is not worth living. There is no joy.

Inner Acceptance

Becoming aware of your automatic thinking and core beliefs is the first part of discovering how your thinking leads to your behavior. Suppose you selectively rely too much on automatic negative thinking. In that case, you will notice that you filter out the good elements and focus hard on the bad ones. Just because you believe something or feel a certain way does not mean that it is true. Feelings are not facts, so they say. Gaining awareness through inner dialogue and harnessing your wise self are instrumental skills when learning to reframe your thoughts or beliefs.

The first step in reframing your thoughts is listening to your self-limiting thoughts and identifying the ones that block you, just like you learned in the previous chapters. Determining whether your thoughts and beliefs help or hinder you is a very critical component of gaining and accepting the need for a new belief. Reframing your thoughts or beliefs requires you to create alternative thoughts that are constructive. They must be realistic, and you must avoid seeing them as fake affirmations that have no meaning to you.

Your negative thinking styles did not miraculously appear overnight. In some cases, they developed and conditioned you over the years, making it hard to take an objective perspective of the beliefs that are hindering you. Your brain plays tricks on you—not intentionally, but by creating mental shortcuts that make you more and more selective about what you pay attention to. These shortcuts are what enable automatic thinking, and it's so automatic that sometimes, we might react emotionally out of impulse because our brains have been wired to be that "efficient." Thoughts and feelings hook us into our emotions, and we respond to them in rigid and inflexible ways that have problematic effects (Harris, 2019).

Validating these initial feelings, exploring inner dialogue, and then reframing these thoughts is paramount to our success in embracing our inner mind. Stop and listen to what's going on in your mind before you react to something. What's the story going on in your head? Is that thought moving you closer or away from the outcome you hope for? Taking what you've learned from earlier chapters, once you've taken steps to validate and explore these inner thoughts, search for the most prominent one that gets you stuck in an emotionally charged situation the most, and reframe it. Don't try to avoid, fight, or stop it. Roll up your sleeves and do the work to repair it.

Anytime we try to fight with our feelings, it is like we are stuck in quicksand. I love the quicksand metaphor because the more you kick frantically to try and get out of the quicksand, the further you sink. However, when you stop kicking and fighting back and allow yourself to relax, you become more focused on making the deliberate actions that will save your life and get you out of the quicksand. Getting out of the quicksand allows you to feel focused and ready to respond with logic rather than react from emotion.

If you go to the gym once, can you expect yourself to be on the stage of the next body-building competition the next day? Of course not! It takes practice, commitment and persistence. Reframing your thoughts requires you to turn inward into a calmer state of mind that helps you to focus and problem-solve. Practicing all of the skills

Inner Acceptance

included in this book, especially the reframing piece, takes time and practice. You'll find there are days when nothing seems to work, and that's okay. Remind yourself that you're learning and you're putting forth a new effort that will grow and shape your life daily.

You have the power within you to experience the change you want to see. Trust this process. Allow yourself the time that you need to work through these areas. It may be a good idea to write these self-limiting thoughts down on a piece of paper. Use the Three-Step Restart Technique to calm your mind, then return to the piece of paper and write down a new thought that is healthier and believable. If you get stuck, you can always close your eyes and turn to your wise self for words of wisdom.

You'll have good days and bad days. You'll try out some of the techniques, and they may not turn out the way you had hoped, but the awfulness won't have the same painful sting it did before, because you are gaining an inner awareness and an inner acceptance of yourself. I challenge you to take this information and try it out. If the outcome doesn't fit with your expectation, look back at what you did, and learn from the experience. Perhaps, you create an alternative thought, and it doesn't click. Evolve it. Change it up. Go online and research positive affirmations or instructions on how to have healthy self-talk to spark your creativity. You do not, however, want to stuff it away or ignore it.

If you find that you're becoming frustrated, take a break. Set a timer on your phone for 10 minutes, and practice the mindfulness that you learned in this book. It is easy to ruminate in your frustrations and allow them to ruin your day. Take charge of your day.

A great question to ask yourself during your inner dialogue or self-talk is, "If I continue to think this way, will it help me to live a life of meaning and overall contentment?" By holding on to those thoughts, are they helping you to be the person you want to be and live the life you want to live? If the answer is no, then ask, "Is there a different way that I could be responding to this situation that will create the outcome that is in alignment with my goals?"

REFRAME Your Story

How do you reframe thoughts? First, you must realize that your initial negative or unwanted thoughts don't just go away. They will always be there. The only solution is to have a better survival strategy for when they do reappear. Here is the REFRAME method I use to help my clients develop this kind of strategy. Use the REFRAME technique after you've validated your inner experience and had inner dialogue, as described in the previous chapter. Here are the key steps:

> **R**—Realize psychological pain is normal.
>
> **E**—Explore alternative ways of your present situation or thought.
>
> **F**—Focus on what's most meaningful for you (goals/outcome).
>
> **R**—Remember the consequences and costs of old behavioral patterns or thoughts.

Inner Acceptance

A—Accept the reality of your problems.

M—Make a commitment to change your thinking and behavioral responses.

E—Expect your thinking to become healthier if you are observant rather than entangled in your emotions.

Realize. The first step in the process is to realize that psychological pain is normal (Hayes, 2005). Although we do everything we possibly can to avoid pain or emotional discomfort, the inner pain we feel must be validated. When you experience emotional discomfort that really hurts, you should go ahead and feel through that. It's OK! If you want to scream, scream. I would discourage you from punching things, but you get the point.

Explore. Become curious about new ways of thinking or behaving. You can do this by asking yourself, "Is there a way for the part that is blocking me right now to step aside so that I can focus on this situation more objectively?" Once the undesired parts that are bubbling up within you step to the side, you will experience a state of calm and focus. Then ask yourself some or all of these questions:

- Is there an alternative way that I can see this problem?
- Is there something more comforting that I can say to myself that demonstrates self-compassion?
- What evidence do I have that makes this thought true?

Attempt to seek a different way of perceiving the issue by gathering the evidence against your initial reaction.

Focus. What is most meaningful to us, like your family or your life's purpose, can often get lost when we are dealing with hardships in life. Identify what is most essential for you in gaining a positive mindset for that situation. What goal or outcome do you hope to achieve? How can you behave in such a way that will give you the desired goal? If your goal is to be explosive and to lash out at yourself or others, that is clearly your personal choice. However, it may be beneficial to think about how your reaction to others is creating a connection or causing disconnection. Better yet, how is your inner dialogue creating a connection or causing disconnection within yourself? How does your inner dialogue prevent you from being a caring person toward others? Are you tired of feeling miserable, inadequate and defective? If the answer is yes, find meaning in your experience.

If this is difficult, start by reviewing your values. Values are your guiding light and will help you when you're stuck. If you are unsure about your values, here is a list to give you some ideas:

Dependability	Being a team player
Reliability	Tolerance
Loyalty	Transparency
Commitment	Integrity
Open-mindedness	Humor
Consistency	Courage
Honesty	Fairness
Efficiency	Faith
Innovation	Generosity
Creativity	

Inner Acceptance

Identifying with your values relates to reframing because it means taking something that you know to be true and turning that into a new positive belief for yourself. So, instead of allowing your failure part to hold you back from doing something you want to do, reframe it into a value such as, "I realize there are times when I get scared and want to give up, but I know that I also have a courageous part of me that lives within me that I can use right now." There are many other examples, but validate your unwanted part and reframe it with a value so it can start playing a new role for you.

Remember. To steer clear of your old behavioral patterns and thoughts, remind yourself of their consequences and costs. You already know exactly what happens when you act out in certain ways—you have a long history proving that. If you keep up with the same cycles, you're not shifting your mindset or changing for the better. Remembering what happens if you keep up those older behaviors will encourage you to continue forward by thinking and behaving differently.

Accept. There's that word again! But it's key. To make a meaningful change in your life, you have to accept the reality of your problems. Let's be real here. There will be times when there is nothing you can say or do that will change the situation. Let yourself know that it is OK. Validate the fact that it is an ongoing problem and remind yourself that you're doing your best to continue to work on it, and hopefully, in the future, there will be incremental changes. If there are no changes, accept the reality that those particular situations simply will not change and move on. Don't dwell on them. Move on, and move forward.

Make a commitment. To change your thinking and behavioral response toward your goal, you have to commit. Once you've decided there is an alternate way of seeing the situation, commit to adopting that new behavioral response. Encourage yourself and know that by changing a particular response or type of self-talk, you are moving toward your goals and expecting change for the better. Making the commitment to change your behavior and thinking in the face of adversity helps you to stay in control of your mindset rather than losing control.

Expect. Your thinking can become healthier if you expect the change to come to fruition. Be observant of your emotions as you make this change, but don't fight them. To be observant is to imagine you are watching a scene in a movie. You can imagine watching the story unfold as you expect greater things to happen. A good example of this is if you are working toward a degree and there is a part of you that wants to give up. Close your eyes and imagine yourself on stage, receiving your diploma. Feel the excitement in your blood as you're handed the diploma and the sense of pride and accomplishment. Expect that to happen!

Every time you change your thinking, you are rewiring your brain. When your brain rewires, it starts conditioning itself to new responses, thoughts, and behaviors. Have the inner confidence to do the tough work and dare to act differently, freeing you from the emotional dysregulation that hinders you. Expect that by behaving differently, you will see different results. Expect that greater things are on the horizon. You'll learn more about expectations in the next chapter.

Inner Acceptance

When using the REFRAME technique, be sure to consult with your wise self if you find yourself getting stuck or unable to come up with a different solution. I tell my clients to experiment with their thoughts and try them out. Self-doubt always sets in and tries to prevent you from taking new action. But don't give in to that criticism. Just do it. Try it. You'll learn from it either way. If the outcome didn't turn out the way you had hoped, just say, "Oh well. That didn't happen the way I wanted, but what did I learn from this? How can I try something different next time?"

Reframing your thoughts helps you to realize the control and power that you have within you. With all of the wonderful things you've learned so far, you now have access to inner acceptance, that which provides the key to the door of your inner power. Accessing that power is exactly what will change your life.

Barbara's Story

This brings me to a story about one of my patients, Barbara, who thought she was defective because her parents abandoned her at a young age. Forced to live with uncaring relatives, Barbara grew up believing that she was unlovable, inadequate, and worthless because of these childhood experiences. Not only was she abandoned by her parents, but the relatives who took care of her criticized her often and told her she would never amount to anything. Although she was on the honor roll and did well in sports, it was never quite good enough for her relatives. There was no encouragement, no pat on the back—nothing. As an adult, the automatic thoughts and core beliefs she developed over time caused her pain at work and in intimate relationships. The constant feeling of not being good enough resulted in not only anxiety but also depression.

Before any major project, Barbara's anxiety would kick in, and she feared that her final product would be rejected by her boss. Her fear caused her to lose sleep at night and she imagined her future being desolate and lonely. These thoughts would trigger her depression. She felt the future was hopeless, so she disconnected from her friends and relationships, which only added to her loneliness. The vicious cycle continued.

During therapy, Barbara became aware of her self-defeating thoughts and their genesis. She realized that experiencing a bad situation did not mean she was terrible. Just because her relatives could not validate her strengths didn't mean that she couldn't validate them for herself. She learned how to open her perspective and see the reality before her eyes that she was lovable and capable of love. She learned how self-compassion enabled her to heal from the painful past and observe, more clearly, the love and abundance that surrounded her. Barbara realized it took a significant amount of strength to endure the situations she faced as a young child and finding that inner courage empowered her.

Her negative thinking and core beliefs were replaced during therapy by using the REFRAME technique, which provided the liberation he needed to release herself from the bondage of her past. She chose to have self-compassion and heal from the past because feeling miserable every day was neither the way she wanted to live her life nor was it the example she wanted to set for

Inner Acceptance

her daughter. So she made different choices about her automatic thinking by accepting them just as thoughts and replacing them with new ones that better aligned with her values and goals. She began telling herself that she was loved and started looking within herself for evidence of that fact. She was able to live more presently in the moment and finally smell the roses, becoming a more loving and present mother and wife. She even got promoted at work.

You can change your thinking and have self-compassion. It just takes effort to find it, believe in it, and live it. When you do, the chances that you can rewire your brain become greater. Rewiring the brain means you are conditioning it to think differently and permanently because it is creating new pathways with every revised thought. These new thoughts are embedded in the brain because of the new emotion that is attached to that response. When you think differently, you feel differently. As someone wise once said, "Your thoughts can be a big hug or a punch in the gut. You choose."

Chapter 9:
Great Expectations

Evolution has shaped our minds so that we are almost inevitably destined to suffer psychologically: to compare, evaluate and criticize ourselves; to focus on what we're lacking; to be dissatisfied with what we have; and to imagine all sorts of frightening scenarios, most of which will never happen. No wonder humans find it hard to be happy!
—Russ Harris

Learning how to sustain everything that you've learned for yourself from this book takes effort. The final stage of continuing the work you've been doing is to focus on what I like to call the TRUST method. You have to trust that your expectations and

Inner Acceptance

outcomes will change. Having higher expectations and optimism about your future is essential in enabling you to move forward from the past.

Inner acceptance motivates you to be the person that you've always dreamed of being. It means finding worth in yourself instead of others. With inner acceptance, you can assert yourself differently and say no when you need to say no—and not feel so guilty about it. Give yourself a strong inner hug and tell yourself that you're going to be OK no matter what challenges you face and that you are loved, not because of validation you receive from others, but because the one person who loves you most is YOU. And no, this isn't narcissism. This is inner acceptance, the core of self-care.

Expect that you are capable of handling anything that you face. When you learn that you can expect great things to happen, they will. It's as simple as that. Create the expectation that no matter the outcome, you are going to learn something significant about yourself. Expect that you will always have the ability to get yourself into a mindset that is loving, healing, and productive. Practice having positive expectations. When you have doubt, validate and replace it with a more optimistic thought.

Your brain is an expectation machine (Vance, 2016), but how those expectations are framed is key. While fear may be the first reaction to something you don't expect, you always have the option to move toward hope and resume your work. And this is the final step in the process of inner acceptance: creating the expectation that the problem you face will be resolved. You can create this expectation by asking yourself, "If I were more focused on what I want to experience or on what I want an outcome to be, how would I behave differently?" Asking this question invites you to use your problem-solving abilities. You can then start to expect that you will act differently. You will expect not to act from anger, but to act from a calm state in which you can be in control of your behavior and make better decisions for yourself, which ultimately impacts your outcomes.

Once you've started thinking about your desired outcomes, then begin to imagine yourself acting in the desired way. Go ahead and thank your unwanted parts for teaching you valuable lessons. Remember that life can be better, and it's not that difficult to realize that. All you need to do is close your eyes, focus on your breath, reflect on your emotional state, have some inner dialogue and reframing, and then imagine your outcome being different. When you open your eyes, you'll notice that you feel different. Undesirable emotions or parts will still be around you—they always will—but they just won't be as intense anymore. Again, the purpose is not to stop the unwanted parts or thoughts or suppress them, but rather to feel them, validate them as they are, and replace them with a more powerful and positive image of the moment.

Begin to imagine how you will be making different choices by simply being able to think and behave differently. Imagine yourself being calm and collected during those turbulent times. You'll feel more in control and then slow down or even stop the cycle of guilt and shame. You can create a new story or outcome because

Inner Acceptance

you can and will experience life differently. You will begin embracing and recognizing how to offer self-love to the "bad" parts of your behavior and appreciate them for the messages they are trying to teach you.

More importantly, expect forgiveness to come. You can forgive yourself for not always knowing what you are doing. Permit yourself to be you. If you look back now and cringe, remind yourself that you were releasing feelings in those ways because you didn't know any alternatives. Your mind had to figure out its own way of dealing with those emotions. So be kind to yourself and forgive the younger you for not knowing any better at the time.

Just because you've had inner dialogue and inner acceptance does not mean that these memories and parts never come back into your mind. They most certainly will, but they won't cripple you as they did in the past. When they do enter your mind, you'll have a strategy. You can sustain your inner healing by following this method:

T—Trust in yourself.

R—Resilience is a part of you.

U—Uplift your mood with new thoughts.

S—Surround yourself with significance.

T—Take time for self-care.

Trust in yourself. Always. You've done some incredible work through this book. You found the courage to have an inner dialogue with some of the most difficult things from your past. You've found ways to be compassionate toward yourself. Surely, you can see that you can trust yourself! You need to be able to trust yourself, just like your parts need to be able to trust you. With the affirmation guidelines you've created for yourself, add this one to the list. No matter what, whether you fail or succeed, you have to have trust that you will be able to handle whatever is in front of you in a calm and focused way. Trust in yourself and ask the parts that block or distract you to step aside so you can regain your focus, knowing full well that you are way better at making good decisions when you are in a calm state of mind.

Resilience is a part of you. It takes a lot of inner strength to experience all that you have experienced through this book. You've been able to pick yourself up and keep moving, even when it felt like there was no safe solution. You faced uncertainty and you prevailed. Always know that resilience is what helps you to stay motivated, determined and powerful. You can access your inner resilience anytime you wish by using the REFRAME method or by accessing your wise self.

Uplift your mood with new thoughts. If you find that a specific affirmation isn't working for you anymore, create a new one. There are times when our thoughts can become stale. Go inward again and find out what has changed and call upon your wise self to give you direction toward new meaning and new thoughts. Once you cultivate the new thought, you will notice your

Inner Acceptance

mood shifting toward being more optimistic and hopeful.

Surround yourself with significance. Remember that you are good enough—always. Anytime you notice a self-defeating thought, validate it and then remind it that you are enough and that you're doing your best. Never try to push the thought away. Also, know that you cannot defeat fear by overthinking. Always acknowledge it and say, "Okay, that was just a thought," and then refocus on what's going on in the present. Go back into your mind with your wise self and remember all the wonderful positive qualities that you have to reinforce your significance.

This means doing the things that offer you that sense of significance. Whether it is applying for that promotion, being present with your family, or going back to school and expanding your knowledge. Whatever helps you to be and feel significant, immerse yourself in it. Others around you will notice a shift in your behavior once all your inner tension is released. You may even find that others will be drawn to your inner strength and you might also be able to help them in some way. Maybe even recommend this book to them.

Take time for self-care. Every day, save a few minutes to be grateful and mindful. Stop and smell the roses. If you're allergic, then smell something else! Do the things that you want to do. Take risks. Go to the gym. Go do what you want to do. Read a book. Take a walk. Go on a minivacation. Be spontaneous. Just be. Just live. Just love.

I had a client, Mike, who was overwhelmed by his demanding job and with being a new father. This feeling was causing him to explode in frustration at his wife and he wanted help. Mike laughed at the idea of self-care and immediately dismissed the idea because he claimed he was too busy. But I challenged him in this self-limiting thought. I had him imagine taking the time for self-care and considering how that would help him to be a wonderful father and a loving husband.

Then, Mike's wise self entered the picture and suggested how he could create time for self-care, redefining the issue for him. Self-care did not mean that he had to become involved in some hobby that he didn't have time for anyway. Self-care meant being present in the moment and noticing the small joys in his life—his child's eyes and hair and the precious moments his wife spent comforting or playing with their child.

Mike redefined what self-care meant to him. Self-care meant that he could take the time to be fully present in the moment with his wife and child. By purposefully seeking the positive details of the moment, he realized that he could find peace. By being more present in the moment, he was not missing out on the little things that could bring him true joy.

Self-care is a huge part of helping you stay well, and it's the key indicator of self-love. You need time for yourself to have inner dialogue. You need to take time for yourself to do the things that you want to do and feel like life is worth living. Life is full of beautiful things that are waiting for you to grab hold of and run with. Once you've learned how to be fully present in your thoughts

Inner Acceptance

and your reality, inner acceptance can energize you. Get creative with your self-care. Self-care doesn't mean that you have to go out and purchase a gym membership. Self-care could be as simple as being fully present in the world around you, even if it takes a second. This concept will help you to sustain everything you've learned in this book.

Chapter 10:
Seeking Further Guidance

My expectations were reduced to zero when I was 21.
Everything since then has been a bonus.
—Stephen Hawking

The hidden yet obvious secret to living a happy life is assuming your problems will one day be resolved and then working toward resolving them. This usually means making different choices, which requires imagining how you might behave differently and recognizing and acknowledging the lessons your "bad" parts are trying to teach you. Remember, just because something feels a certain way doesn't mean it is a fact. From this inner self-awareness and desire to change, you become the author of your story, allowing

Inner Acceptance

you to take the pen and write how your inner world narrates your life events.

Still, you might want or need more help to reach this point. If you find the ideas in this book intriguing, but you need a little more support, I encourage you to find a therapist that specializes in parts therapy, hypnosis, or internal family systems. This book is meant to complement the work you do with your therapist, even if they do not specialize in the techniques just mentioned. It is one thing to understand concepts at a conscious level, but it's a whole different experience when someone can help you tap into and activate the unconscious mind. That is when true healing happens.

There are also other excellent self-help books that I highly recommend for furthering your knowledge. *Freedom from Your Inner Critic* by Early and Weiss, for example, is very valuable because it goes into more detail about how to have a dialogue with your inner-critic parts. It even includes some journaling exercises that are very beneficial. The authors did a great job of providing additional details on how you can use your imagination and bring the stories of your parts to life so that you can understand them better. When your brain can imagine the story, you will experience longer-lasting relief from whatever was blocking you.

Although I did not discuss it in detail in this book, there is also a great book by Mona Barbera on understanding your inner world and your significant other's inner world. *Bring Yourself to Love* helps couples understand each other better and learn how to love each other at a more meaningful level. It also has journaling exercises to help provoke thought and provide additional insight into what's happening in your inner world, which ultimately impacts your relationship.

An excellent book related to mindfulness is Andy Puddicombe's *The Headspace Guide to Meditation and Mindfulness*. Puddicombe brings to life the ancient practice of meditation and breaks it down in an easy-to-read format so you can implement or apply meditation concepts right away. I read this book on a trip to Hawaii, and it helped me with anxiety during the flight. The book can also be supplemented by an app (Headspace) that Puddicombe developed, and it has helped many of my clients.

Okay, enough with the books! Another important paradox to the concept of expectations explored in Chapter 9 is our unmet expectations. Unmet expectations tend to trigger our undesirable parts in ways that we may later regret. When a loved one is not living up to our expectations, we become resentful and frustrated. Imagine a couple in an argument because one partner needed something done in a certain way. Yet, they assumed their partner knew exactly how to be and do according to their wishes. That kind of argument stems from a lack of communication. The partner who initiated the request failed to clearly state their expectations. Yet, they became frustrated and lashed out when those uncommunicated expectations weren't meant. Perhaps, they even balled other particles of their history into one, and it lobs itself in their mind with "She always does that, and it pisses me off," when in reality, that is an untrue statement.

Inner Acceptance

This kind of miscommunication happens all the time. Hannah came to me for guidance on how to resolve the internalized resentment she had for her husband. Hannah was working full time, and her husband was unemployed. When she would come home, the house would be cluttered and in total disarray. She began to feel resentful toward her husband because he wasn't helping around the house. She expected that he would complete some of the chores so that by the time she returned home from work, she could relax. Instead, she'd have to clean the house herself, and her inner story told her, "He doesn't love me enough to even clean the house for us. He is lazy." Deep resentment built because of her unmet expectations, creating a gap between the two of them. In therapy, she identified how her unmet expectations were causing her to harbor negative feelings toward her husband.

To resolve this issue, she needed to be transparent with her husband and communicate to him what her expectations were of him and how she felt unloved and unappreciated. This is called setting boundaries. Setting boundaries with someone means you communicate to them what you will and will not tolerate. It's also important to share what consequences are in store if someone violates your boundaries. When Hannah learned how to communicate her expectations and how she felt, she noticed a considerable improvement in his behavior. He was more attentive and started helping out more around the house. They grew closer because she found it easier to explain to her husband how he could help her. With better communication, they could show more love toward each other.

If you find yourself experiencing hardships because you are failing to communicate your expectations healthily and lovingly to others, reconsider how your behavior is contributing to the disconnection. Identify which needs are going unmet, and hone in on the story you tell yourself about the situation. Then clearly communicate your expectations. By failing to share what your unmet expectations are, you will continue the cycle of negative inner dialogue and disconnection. Work toward finding solutions and create an expectation in your mind that change is possible.

Conclusion

The solutions are there. If only we knew how to reach inside our minds to find them.
—Marty Lerman

Learning inner acceptance has enabled you to change the lens you use to view life. You've learned how childhood experiences shape your immature inner dialogue. You've learned how to heal your inner dialogue with self-compassion and by reframing thoughts. Now, the true test is challenging yourself to confront your self-limiting beliefs and thoughts without judgment and practice the skills included in this book.

Go at your own pace. There is no hurry. There's no light switch you can just flick for everything to, voila, suddenly be amazing. It takes commitment and work to obtain results. Mere understanding of the material presented in this book doesn't do much. You have to put it into practice. Your initial instinct may be to ignore the internal challenges this book directs you to face, but remember the tea kettle metaphor. We all experience struggles that are difficult to face head-on, but we need to face them, or the kettle will start screeching. It takes a lot of courage to do this work. I promise that when you practice the simple steps outlined in this book, the pieces of the puzzle start falling into place, and you'll naturally begin taking care of yourself.

Motivate yourself and affirm that you can do this. Read this book again when you get stuck. Find a relative or a friend to share the book with, and grow together. There are a variety of ways to use the materials in this book, so start anywhere you like. There is no right or wrong way to do this. If you find yourself getting stuck in a painful memory of the past, set a timer for 5 minutes. When the timer buzzes to alert you that your time is up, find the list of values in Chapter 8. Pick one value from the list and focus on it to help you to move forward with a growth mindset. Better yet, purchase my gratitude journal, Gratitude Sprinkles: How to Sprinkle that Sh*t Everywhere and Live a Bomb-@ss Life. Inside, you will find content prompts to assist you in starting and ending your day with thoughtfulness, meaning and gratitude.

If you find that there are some deeper layers to your story, I encourage you to see a counselor or hypnotherapist to assist you in overcoming your internal challenges. You can leverage this book to supplement what you're learning and experiencing in therapy.

Inner Acceptance

Find freedom in knowing that you can change. Yes, it takes work. Yes, some moments will rise to the surface repeatedly in your future. However, you have a strategy this time. Unhappiness is something that you choose for yourself. Implement an approach that enables you to make choices that offer significance in your life. There is only one life to live. Start living your life according to your wishes.

The solutions you seek are already within your mind, ready to be unlocked by the content of this book. Your unconscious mind will go to work for you and help you to accomplish your inner desires. Do not expect perfection. Expect that you can handle anything that comes your way one day at a time, even during times of adversity or despair. Sit confidently, knowing that uncertainty is certain at times. Sit quietly with yourself when you need comfort or support. After all, you are who you can count on the most, even if there are times when you are critical and deflated.

Contemplate your possibilities in life. The past does not define you. Instead, it helps to shape you into a strong, capable and worthy person. The lessons of your history will become a testimony for others if you choose to impart your inner wisdom to them. Your story can and will inspire others.

By reading this book, you have now discovered the magnificent and powerful advantage of true inner acceptance. Practice wholeheartedly on a daily basis. Reach out to professionals for help. Try to incorporate the parts of this book that resonate with you the most.

In closing, I want to remind you that I have posted many free resources and guided meditations for you to continue your journey of inner acceptance on my website at www.inneracceptance.com.

Share this with your loved ones and friends. Together, build a community of resilience and acceptance for all.

References

Backus, W., & Chapian, M. (2000). Telling Yourself the Truth. Grand Rapids, MI: Bethany House Publishers.

Barbera, M. (2016). Bring Yourself to Love. Providence, RI: Dos Monos Press.

Brown, B. (2019). Dare to Lead. New York, NY: Penguin Random House, LLC.

Emmerson, G. (2007). Ego State Therapy. Bethel, CT: Crown House Publishing Ltd.

Harris, R. (2019). ACT Made Simple (2ndnd ed.). Oakland, CA: New Harbinger Publications.

Hayes, S. C. (2005). Get Out of Your Mind & Into Your Life. Oakland, CA: New Harbinger Publications.

Holmes, T., & Holmes, L. (2007). Parts Work An Illustrated Guide to Your Inner Life. Kalamazoo, MI: Winged Heart Press.

Hunter, R. (2005). Hypnosis for Inner Conflict Resolution. Williston, VT: Crown House Publishing Ltd.

Lerman, M. (2013). Mind Shift Your Mind Doesn't Have to Suck. Bloomington, IN: AuthorHouse.

Missildine, W. (1963). Your Inner Child of the Past. New York, NY: Simon and Schuster.

Nongard, R. K., & Woods, K. T. (2018). Reframing Hypnotherapy. Scottsdale, AZ: Peachtree Professional Education, Inc.

Puddicombe, A. (2011). The Headspace Guide to Meditation & Mindfulness. New York, NY: St. Martin's Press.

Schwartz, R. C., & Sweezy, M. (2020). Internal Family Systems Therapy (Second ed.). New York, NY: The Guilford Press.

Vance, E. (2016). Suggestible You. Washington, DC: National Geographic Partners, LLC.

Woititz, J. (1983). Adult Children of Alcoholics. Deerfield Beach, FL: Health Communications, Inc.

www.ingramcontent.com/pod-product-compliance
Lightning Source LLC
Chambersburg PA
CBHW031121080526
44587CB00011B/1066